Especially for

Barbarita

From

Ramirez Family

Date

2/14/2023

D1089571

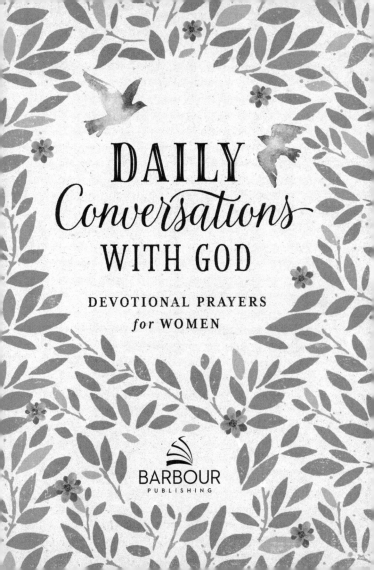

DAILY
Conversations
WITH GOD

DEVOTIONAL PRAYERS
for WOMEN

BARBOUR
PUBLISHING

Print ISBN 978-1-63609-296-6

Cover design: Greg Jackson, Thinkpen Design

Published by Barbour Publishing, Inc., 1810 Barbour Drive, Uhrichsville, Ohio 44683, www.barbourbooks.com

Our mission is to inspire the world with the life-changing message of the Bible.

Member of the
Evangelical Christian
Publishers Association

Day 1

COME CLOSER, BELOVED

In him and through faith in him we may
approach God with freedom and confidence.

EPHESIANS 3:12 NIV

Dear Lord, You are the God of the universe, and yet You ask me to come closer. I can't stand in Your presence, yet You ask me to approach with freedom and confidence. It's all because of Jesus, Lord, that I can do this! I praise You for the great gift of Your Son, who allows me this access to You, my Creator. I am so small, but I long to know You better. I am so weak, but I know You have power to spare. Help me to come to You again and again. In Jesus' precious name, amen.

Day 2

IN YOUR PRESENCE THIS DAY

"If my people, who are called by my name, will humble themselves and pray and seek my face and turn from their wicked ways, then I will hear from heaven."

2 CHRONICLES 7:14 NIV

Dear Father, I thank You that Your ear is always listening for the cries of Your people. You are always listening for my voice, and You know it out of billions of others. My words are not just spoken to the empty air, but You give them Your attention. Forgive me for my sins today, Lord, for they are many. I rest under Your mercy.

Day 3

EVERYTHING IS POSSIBLE

Abba, Father, all things are possible unto thee.
MARK 14:36 KJV

How amazing, Lord—my Father is the Creator of the universe! Your infinite creativity formed the beauty of the earth and the intricacies of life. I know I can rest assured in Your strength, in Your might, in Your abilities. There's nothing on heaven or on earth that You can't handle. Forgive me when I try to take things into my own hands. Since You made the world and everything in it, I know You can take care of my small life!

Day 4

JOINT HEIRS WITH CHRIST

*For ye have not received the spirit of bondage
again to fear; but ye have received the Spirit of
adoption, whereby we cry, Abba, Father. The
Spirit itself beareth witness with our spirit, that
we are the children of God: and if children, then
heirs; heirs of God, and joint-heirs with Christ.*

ROMANS 8:15–17 KJV

Thank You, Lord, for adopting me into Your family,
for making me Your heir, just as Jesus is. There's nothing I can do to deserve this favor or this acceptance.
Your grace is all-sufficient. I now call Jesus my brother,
and together we share in Your amazing glory!

Day 5

RECEIVING JESUS

*But as many as received him, to them
gave he power to become the sons of God,
even to them that believe on his name.*

JOHN 1:12 KJV

Lord, I believe in Your name. Help me every day to believe still more. Take away the doubts and insecurities that the world shouts at me every day. Keep my eyes firmly focused on You, even when troubles come. Keep my ears attuned to Your voice, especially when I am tempted to listen to other voices. I welcome You into my heart—to make a home there now and forever.

Day 6

THE ONE WHO IS

*Who is like the L*ORD *our God, who dwells on high?*

PSALM 113:5 NKJV

Heavenly Father, today I'm grateful for all You are—the God who is, the God of the living, the great I AM. Your character is unchanging. You are the epitome of perfect holiness and love. Because of who and all You are, I believe and trust in You. Your truthfulness is indisputable, and Your power is established. Not just for the majestic works by Your hand but for the pure glory of Your nature—I worship You today. Amen.

Day 7

GRACE FOR EVERYTHING

But he gives us more grace.

JAMES 4:6 NIV

Father, I'm thankful for Your *grace*—Your unmerited favor to me through Jesus Christ and that special strength You give Your children in times of need, trial, and temptation. If not for Your grace, I wouldn't even be able to approach You. Thank You for extending favor to me: forgiving my sins and adopting me into Your family. And thank You so much for that extra dose of perseverance that You keep giving to me in tough situations. I'm so thankful Your resource center will never experience a shortage. I praise You today for grace. Amen.

Day 8

THE LORD ALMIGHTY

And [I] will be a Father unto you, and ye shall be my sons and daughters, saith the Lord Almighty.

2 Corinthians 6:18 kjv

You, God, can do all things for You are almighty, all-powerful. Because You are my Father, I know I can trust You to handle each and every aspect of my life. Show me new ways that I can rely on You to work in a mighty way in my life. I trust You with my past, my present, and my future. You are God, and I am not—and I am thankful that's the way it is.

Day 9

ARISE AND GO

*The word which came to Jeremiah from the Lord,
saying: "Arise and go down to the potter's house,
and there I will cause you to hear My words."*

JEREMIAH 18:1–2 NKJV

So many times, Lord, I feel the urge to drop to my
knees and pray. Yet I don't. Embarrassment, busyness,
a dirty floor—they can all stop me from heeding Your
call. Yet I praise You that You keep calling my name
again and again. Please help me to trust You enough
to stop what I am doing when I hear Your call. I am on
my knees now, my King. I am listening to Your voice.

Day 10

THE LIVING FOSSIL

You are an epistle of Christ. . .written not with ink but by the Spirit of the living God, not on tablets of stone but on tablets of flesh, that is, of the heart.

2 Corinthians 3:3 nkjv

Lord, You have preserved Your Word for thousands of years. It is uncorrupted, it is unchanged, it has not been forgotten. Like an animal buried and hammered into rock by time and pressure, it has come down to us, yet it is not fossilized: it lives! You chiseled Your law into rock for Moses, but now Your Word is written in our hearts. And we too will live uncorrupted and unforgotten but, thanks be to You, *changed*. Amen.

LUTHER, WESLEY, CROSBY, ETC.

*Let the word of Christ dwell in you richly in
all wisdom; teaching and admonishing one
another in psalms and hymns and spiritual songs,
singing with grace in your hearts to the Lord.*

COLOSSIANS 3:16 KJV

Dear God, I don't know where I'd be tonight without
the great hymns of the faith that have resounded in
my head since I was a girl. Thank You for that legacy
of music and poetry and for what You have taught
me through meditating on those lines. I praise You
for the men and women who penned the lyrics and
music that still minister to Christians today. Thank
You for the hymns that kept my heart tuned to You
even when I thought I was running far away. Great is
Thy faithfulness! Amen.

Day 12

A FATHER'S MERCY

I will be his father, and he shall be my son:
and I will not take my mercy away from him.

1 Chronicles 17:13 kjv

Thank You, Lord, that You will never take Your mercy away from me. No matter how many times I let You down, I can always count on You to pick me up. I cannot understand this gift, but I am thankful for it, Father. Please show me ways to extend mercy to others in my life—especially to those whom the world may deem as "unlovable." Because the truth is, God, I know that some days I too am unlovable.

Day 13

IN THE INNER ROOM

"But you, when you pray, go into your inner room, close your door and pray to your Father who is in secret, and your Father who sees what is done in secret will reward you."

<small>Matthew 6:6 NASB</small>

Dear God, You know how often I pray and how often I *don't*. You know that sometimes I use it as a weapon. "Lord, give me patience!" I say in the presence of those who are vexing me. Please forgive me. That is not prayer. And Lord, forgive me for *not* praying. Forgive me for wasting the quiet moments that You give me with things that will be forgotten in eternity. I want to know You now, *here*, even before I am with You forever. Amen.

Day 14

GETTING TO KNOW YOU

We loved you so much, we were delighted to share with you not only the gospel of God but our lives as well.

1 Thessalonians 2:8 niv

Dear Lord, thank You for reminding me today to pray for the people who witnessed to me before I was a believer. I was so ignorant of Your ways, Lord, that I didn't even know that was what they were doing! I thought they were just telling me about their lives, that we were getting to know each other, when really they were introducing me to their Savior. I praise You for how real You were to them and for their example of how sharing our faith is more about *conversation* than conversion. Bless those brave evangelists, Lord, and continue to do Your work through them. Amen.

Day 15

GOD OF ALL COMFORT

*Blessed be God. . .the Father of mercies,
and the God of all comfort.*

2 Corinthians 1:3 kjv

You comfort me, Father, when my heart aches. When everything in my life seems to be going wrong. . . when the world is full of violence and disaster. . . when loss is everywhere I look. . .when hope is dying inside me, Your comfort never fails. Thank You for offering me that constant care in my life. Help me to always extend comfort, care, and compassion to others as well—ultimately leading them to You.

Day 16

I WILL HEAR

"Before they call I will answer; while they are still speaking I will hear."

ISAIAH 65:24 NIV

Dear Lord, I praise You that You are the God who hears. I praise You that You know my heart even before *I* do. I rest in the fact that You are answering my prayer even before I pray. Help me to be more like You, Lord. So often I don't take the time to listen with love to the people around me. And while they are still speaking, I say *no*. I need Your ears and Your heart, Lord. Speak to me and through me. Amen.

Day 17

HERE ARE MY MOTHER AND BROTHERS

Pointing to his disciples, he said, "Here are my mother and my brothers. For whoever does the will of my Father in heaven is my brother and sister and mother."

MATTHEW 12:49–50 NIV

Dear Father, sometimes I feel like I'd do better on a desert island. It's hard to live in community. Our rough edges meet the rough edges of others, and the results are scrapes and sparks and *wounds*. Thank You so much for the pictures You present in the Gospels of Jesus living with His disciples. Lord, nothing teaches me more about what pleases You and what is *possible* than studying how You did it, how You lived and loved and ate and traveled together. Help me think of the people I rub elbows with as *my* disciples, companions, and teachers. Amen.

Day 18

A GODLY CONFIDENCE

Now this is the confidence that we have in Him, that if we ask anything according to His will, He hears us.

1 JOHN 5:14 NKJV

Dear Lord, there are so many things I want. Sometimes I feel like my prayers are just a long list of wishes, as though You're some sort of celestial genie. But I'm so thankful You are not. You don't give me what I want just because I want it. I thank You that You give me only what is in line with Your will for me. So, Lord, show me what that is. Reveal Your will, and show me how and for what You want me to pray.

WHAT MANNER OF LOVE

Behold, what manner of love the Father hath bestowed upon us, that we should be called the sons of God.

1 JOHN 3:1 KJV

A good father protects his children; he loves his children unconditionally; he understands and forgives his children; he provides for his family; he is intimately involved in the lives of those he loves. You are more than a good father, God—You are the *perfect* Father. Remind me, Lord, that *this* is the way You love me. Thank You for loving all of me—unconditionally and without reservation.

Day 20

LITTLE ALTARS ALL OVER

Then let us arise and go up to Bethel, and I will make there an altar to God Who answered me in the day of my distress and was with me wherever I went.

GENESIS 35:3 AMPC

Lord, how easily we forget Your faithfulness. I think *I* would never be like the Israelites, longing for the slave-grown melons and cucumbers of Egypt while following the fire of God through the desert. But my memory is just as short, just as fickle. You knew they needed reminders, so their path was littered with altars and memorials, their calendar marked with feasts and holidays and fasts. *"Don't forget who I Am and what I have done,"* You say. Lord, please show me tangible ways to remember Your faithfulness to me too. Amen.

Day 21

LIGHTS

*That ye may be blameless and harmless,
the sons of God, without rebuke, in the midst
of a crooked and perverse nation, among
whom ye shine as lights in the world.*

PHILIPPIANS 2:15 KJV

Lord, I am grateful that I can claim You as my Father. Because You live in my heart, I am Your representative to the world around me. Thank You for using me for Your purpose, and thank You for filling in the gaps where I am inadequate to do Your work. Make me Your light in the world around me not so I can gain fame for myself but only to proclaim Your awesomeness.

Day 22

GOOD GIFTS

"If you then, being evil, know how to give good gifts to your children, how much more will your Father who is in heaven give what is good to those who ask Him!"

MATTHEW 7:11 NASB

Lord, You are good. You are good! You are a loving, generous God, slow to anger and rich in love. I pray that the riches You offer through Christ Jesus would be visible in my life so that others would be drawn to You. I have nothing to offer them except You, Jesus. But You have so much, and You long to open the storehouses of heaven to us, blessings pressed down and running over. Amen.

Day 23

CHILDREN OF THE RESURRECTION

*Neither can they die any more:
for they are. . .the children of God,
being the children of the resurrection.*

LUKE 20:36 KJV

Because I am Your child, I don't need to be afraid of death. You Yourself conquered death and the grave on Easter morning, and You promise me that Your grace will save me from eternal death as well. How amazing and wonderful and humbling! I am so glad, Lord, for the promise of Your resurrection and the assurance of eternity with You in heaven. Help me to be bold in sharing this wonderful hope with people who have no hope.

Day 24

WITH THIS RING

*For no matter how many promises God
has made, they are "Yes" in Christ.*

2 CORINTHIANS 1:20 NIV

Dear Lord, You are faithful yesterday, today, and tomorrow. I thank You for giving me a husband who exemplifies that enduring faithfulness. Thank You for how he has kept the promises he made to me on our wedding day: promises to love, cherish, protect, and provide. Thank You for his hands that hold my heart so gently; thank You that he is more like Jesus than anyone I have ever known. I praise You for the great gift that he is to me. Thank You for his example of faithful love, and I pray that I would give him only joy, submission, and devotion in return. Amen.

Day 25

ALCHEMY FOR A RAINY DAY

My voice shalt thou hear in the morning,
O LORD; in the morning will I direct my
prayer unto thee, and will look up.

PSALM 5:3 KJV

Dear Lord, it's so dark this morning. I know You've already pushed the sun up over the horizon; it is day, though it doesn't feel like it. I don't want to have to pray this morning, Lord. I just want to be where You are. I don't want to be here, in this gray light, with a longer grayness stretching before me, then darkness again. I want to be with You, walking on streets of gold, with the light of Your glory shining on my face. I long for that endless golden day, Lord. But I am here, and You are not far off. Please come to me, Lord, and shine Your love and light on my heart this morning. Amen.

Day 26

PEACE

Grace unto you, and peace, from God our Father.

2 Thessalonians 1:2 kjv

Thank You, Father, for the gift of Your peace. Help me to remember that Your peace is the only true and lasting rest for my soul—and to always run to You and no other idol in my life. When troubles come my way, please give me an extra dose of Your peace. And when I see others in turmoil, help me to always be ready with a word and an action that will help them seek out Your peace.

Day 27

TWENTY-FOUR

This is the day which the LORD hath made;
we will rejoice and be glad in it.

PSALM 118:24 KJV

I thank You for this day, Lord, with its twenty-four precious, exhausting hours. Only twenty-four. That never seems like enough, yet I'm always glad to fall into bed when they're over. Some hours spent in sleep, some in work, some in eating, some in talking, some in staring out the kitchen window at the trees and sky. How many of those hours do I give to You, Lord? Not even *one*, maybe two on Sundays? Thank You for continuing to remind me that relationships require *time*, and I vow to give You more of each day—each day that is already a gift from You. Amen.

Day 28

FALLING

Cast your cares on the LORD and he will sustain you; he will never let the righteous be shaken.

PSALM 55:22 NIV

Dear Father, we started falling in Eden, and we haven't hit bottom yet. Today I said some things I regret. And the things I didn't say (the things only *You* heard) were even worse. I hurt people I care about, and worse, I hurt You, Lord. I am so sorry. Please forgive me. Please redeem my angry, selfish words. I am so glad that You tell us in Your Word to forgive seventy times seven times because I know that is how many times You will forgive me. Thanks be to Jesus; when I fall, I am falling into Your arms. Amen.

Day 29

THE TIME OF SINGING

*For lo, the winter is past, the rain is over
and gone. The flowers appear on the
earth; the time of singing has come.*

<small>SONG OF SOLOMON 2:11–12 NKJV</small>

Father, the earth is brown and dead now, as hard as
iron and as cold as stone. But I know that life lurks,
waits: seeds that will spring to green life with the
warming sun and a gentle rain, nests that will hold
eggs the color of sky, ponds that will sparkle and sing
with dragonflies and frogs. Thank You for spring, for
the promise of green and new life. And thank You for
heaven, where that fleeting green will never fade and
fall away. Amen.

Day 30

SPIRIT-LED

For as many as are led by the Spirit of God,
they are the sons of God.

ROMANS 8:14 KJV

Father, let Your Spirit lead me in each thing. Let me always look to You for guidance and direction. Keep me away from the temptation of following the paths of other "gods." Make Your Spirit alive and active in my heart so that I might hear Your voice every day, in my every decision, and in my every action. Forgive me when I ignore the movement of Your Spirit. Make Him active in my heart, Lord!

Day 31

THE MISSING "P"

*"For then you will delight in the Almighty
and lift up your face to God."*

JOB 22:26 NASB

Dear Father, today I just want to praise You! I spend so much time repenting (read: *sinning*), asking (complaining), and yielding (pretending not to be so stubborn), and so little time telling You how much I love You. You are merciful, You are awesome, You are holy! You are beyond compare. You are my Maker and sustainer. You saved me! You are light and love and all that is good. Lord, You made *mountains*. And trees that spear the clouds and birds as bright as rainbows and flowers as small and perfect as a baby's fingernail. Who is like You? Amen and amen and amen.

Day 32

THE DAY OF SMALL THINGS

For who hath despised the day of small things? for they shall rejoice.

ZECHARIAH 4:10 KJV

Dear Lord, I ask for thankfulness in the small things. I yearn to see each day as a gift—swathed in sunrise—to be unwrapped. Thank You, Lord, for what You gave me today: for a curl of green leaf unfurling on the winter end of a branch, for a cherry blossom like a snag of fuchsia silk, for scratchy frog songs. Thank You for moments that remind me that ordinary days are really shot through with holiness. I thank You now, Lord, for those gifts and the gifts that I will see *You've already given me* as I learn to live in thankfulness. Amen.

Day 33

EXPECTING MIRACLES

*Then the fire of the L*ORD *fell and consumed the burnt
sacrifice, and the wood and the stones and the dust,
and it licked up the water that was in the trench.*

1 KINGS 18:38 NKJV

Dear God, I come before You today, knowing You are a
God who works miracles. You heal the blind, the lame,
the scarred and leprous, and the demon possessed. You
crack open prison cells, turn night into day, and roll
the ocean up like a scroll. You send down fire from
heaven. You bring the dead back to life. I am no Elijah,
Lord, but I know You love me. Please answer my prayer
today. Work my small miracle. Amen.

Day 34

LIVING WORDS

O Lord, You are my God. I will exalt You, I will praise Your name, for You have done wonderful things; Your counsels of old are faithfulness and truth.

Isaiah 25:1 nkjv

Dear God, Your Word is thousands of years old and tells stories even older. How many books made millennia ago are still useful today? Curious, maybe, or *interesting*, but still practical? Lord, I can't think of even one. We read old poems, histories, and sagas for school assignments or because we want to learn about the past or because they tell good stories, but how many lives have been changed from reading *Beowulf* or *The Canterbury Tales*? Your Word is as true today as when the ink was wet. It is beautiful. It is inspiring. It is rich. It surprises. It sustains. It transforms. I praise the living Word.

Day 35

PEACEMAKERS

Blessed are the peacemakers: for they shall be called the children of God.

MATTHEW 5:9 KJV

Dear Lord, teach me that if I want the world to see me as Your child, then I need to always work for peace in the world around me. Help me resist the temptation to stir up bitterness or anger among my family, friends, and neighbors. Take away angry, jabbing words that may well up in the heat of the moment. Instead, teach me to be a peacemaker, so that others can't help but acknowledge that You are living and active within me.

Day 36

THE WATCHER

The LORD will keep you from all harm—he will watch over your life; the LORD will watch over your coming and going both now and forevermore.

PSALM 121:7–8 NIV

Lord, I'm scared. I'm scared of someone I love getting sick. I'm scared of not having enough money. I'm scared of our country falling apart. I'm scared of being abandoned. I'm scared of hurting the ones I love. I'm scared of stepping on snakes. I'm scared of being laughed at. I'm scared that I'll grow old and die before You return. But mostly I'm scared of never knowing You better than I know You right now. Thank You for that fear, Lord, and how it drives me to my knees again and again. Amen.

Day 31

LOVING OUR ENEMIES

*But love ye your enemies, and do good, and lend,
hoping for nothing again; and your reward shall be
great, and ye shall be the children of the Highest.*

LUKE 6:35 KJV

Heavenly Father, You know I have a hard time loving some of the people in my life. Some of them are downright nasty to me. But Your Word says that You want me to repay evil with good. Remind me that You ask me as Your child to not only love my enemies but to also do them positive, active good without thought of reward. It's not going to be easy, Lord, but with Your help, I can do it.

Day 38

THE DEAD WILL LIVE!

But your dead will live, LORD; their bodies
will rise—let those who dwell in the
dust wake up and shout for joy.

ISAIAH 26:19 NIV

Dear Lord, I was feeling so sad this morning. Maybe it was partly the rain and the gray skies, but I was missing certain people so badly. My dad, my grandmothers, my great-aunts, friends. They are all dead, Lord, and that seems so strange and wrong. They are in the ground, out of sight, out of reach. Thank You for comforting me with the assurance that it *is* wrong, that death was not part of Your plan. And that, ultimately, it will be swallowed up in victory. My dad, my grandmothers, they will wake up and shout for joy. Hallelujah!

Day 39

PRAYING LIKE BREATH

Rejoice always; pray without ceasing.

1 THESSALONIANS 5:16–17 NASB

Lord, You gave me life, and I praise You. You filled my lungs with air from my very first breath, and I praise You. I praise You because I am fearfully and wonderfully made. Forgive me for not always loving this body You have given me like the amazing creation and great gift that it is. Today, Lord, I want to pray to You like I breathe: in and out, all day long. Fill my mouth with Your praise. Let my lips be always whispering Your name. Let my heart beat to the rhythm of Your perfect will. Amen.

Day 40

GOD'S OFFSPRING

For in him we live, and move, and have our being. . .for we are also his offspring.

ACTS 17:28 KJV

The world tells me to be independent, self-sufficient, and to stand on my own two feet. But the truth is that I am intimately connected to the Lord of the universe, and I rely on You for my life, Father. Most days it's a relief that it's not all on me to handle everything. To put it another way, You and I are kinfolk, Lord! I would not exist if it were not for You.

THE WEDDING MARCH

*He who finds a wife finds a good thing,
and obtains favor from the LORD.*

PROVERBS 18:22 NKJV

Dear Father, my kids are all still little and know nothing of romantic desire. They are still in love with me and their father. But I know the day is coming, Lord, when they will transfer their affections to someone else, and I lift those yet-unknown *someones* up to You. Bless their future spouses with faith and wisdom and purity as they wait. I pray that You would help me show my children what marriage can be and that You would hold their hearts, Lord, until You join them with another. Amen.

Day 42

CALL TO ME

*"Call to me and I will answer you and tell you
great and unsearchable things you do not know."*

JEREMIAH 33:3 NIV

Lord of the universe, You know everything; You see
everything; You are everywhere; You are every *time*
and eternal. Lord, sometimes we think that we are so
smart, we people that You *made*. Compared to You,
we are babies one minute old, looking up at the light
and blinking, unable to comprehend anything. But
You want us to grow up, Lord. You long to teach us
everything You know. I yield my heart and mind to
You. Amen.

Day 43

WHO KNOWS?

Beloved, now are we the sons of God,
and it doth not yet appear what we shall be.

1 John 3:2 kjv

Father, I'm grateful for being Your child in this life. I can't even imagine what that will mean in the life to come! Thank You for the hope You have given to me for now and for an unknown future. Although I don't know all the details of what You have in store, I am thankful I can rest secure, knowing You have it all under control.

Day 44

MAKE ME WISER

*If any of you lacks wisdom, let him ask of God,
who gives to all liberally and without reproach,
and it will be given to him.*

JAMES 1:5 NKJV

Dear Father, today I stumbled up against something that calls for Your wisdom. Someone might be in trouble, Lord. But it's a delicate situation, and I might be wrong. I've been wrong before, You know, and stepped out to offer help without Your blessing and just made things worse. I want to be used by You in people's lives, but first I need Your wisdom. I'm no Solomon, Lord, but just like he did, I'm asking for Your wisdom. Thank You that You promise to give it to me freely and generously. And please protect the woman with the bruised cheek. Amen.

Day 45

THE CONFIDENCE OF FIRSTHAND KNOWLEDGE

I've got my eye on the goal, where God is beckoning us onward—to Jesus. I'm off and running, and I'm not turning back.

PHILIPPIANS 3:14 MSG

Lord, it all comes down to knowing You. Who I am, where I'm headed, and what You require of me all depend on who You are. I don't ask for supernatural revelation, Lord (though I wouldn't turn it down). I just ask for a dogged determination to know You better, verse by verse. I ask—beg, really—for a continual filling of Your Spirit so that my eyes and heart are wide open to You. Then I can say *amen* with confidence. And I will: Amen!

Day 46

GOD IS LOVE

*God is love; and he that dwelleth in
love dwelleth in God, and God in him.*

1 John 4:16 KJV

God, let me never forget that You are love—patient,
kind, not envious, not proud, not rude, not self-
seeking, not easily angered, keeping no record of
wrongs. You do not delight in evil, but You rejoice
in the truth. You always protect, trust, hope, and
persevere. Your love will always remain. It is the
greatest thing there is. May I always make my home
within You—within Your love.

Day 47

THE SALVATION OF EVERYONE!

For I am not ashamed of the gospel of Christ: for it is the power of God unto salvation to every one that believeth.

ROMANS 1:16 KJV

Dear God, sometimes I get weary waiting for You. I am not patient about waiting for the things I long for with all my heart. But I know You are patient, Lord. You are waiting. You are waiting for *us*. Oh, thank You, that You won't return until everyone has had a chance to hear the Gospel. Thank You that Your incredible patience and love is greater than our persistent sin. Who can I tell, Lord? Who is near me who hasn't yet heard or understood the Good News? Even so, come, Lord Jesus. Amen.

Day 48

WISDOM AND MIGHT

Blessed be the name of God for ever and ever:
for wisdom and might are his.

DANIEL 2:20 KJV

You, Lord, are all-wise. You make the wisdom of the world look like nothing but foolishness. I will never fully grasp the vastness of Your wisdom, but I am thankful to have that strength in my corner. Scripture says that along with being all-wise, You're all-powerful as well. Speak, and the heavens and the earth are at Your beck and call. No matter how powerful we humans think we are, You are the One who holds it all. Today I "hallow Your name" by relying on Your wisdom and might.

Day 49

LISTEN TO THE MUSIC

The Spirit and the bride say, "Come." And let the one who hears say, "Come." And let the one who is thirsty come; let the one who wishes take the water of life without cost.

REVELATION 22:17 NASB

Dear Father, I'm lifting up a teenager to You tonight who gives You lip service but whose heart doesn't belong to You yet. She knows what to say when Christians are watching, but I know her answers are different when she is in other company. Lord, You are watching her. Remind her of this. Hound her, Lord, until she turns her heart to You. But in this I praise You: she only listens to Christian music. Her soul is yearning for You, whether she knows it or not. Fan that small spark of desire into an eternal *yes*. Amen.

Day 50

THE CHEERLEADER

I can do all things through
Christ who strengthens me.

PHILIPPIANS 4:13 NKJV

Dear Lord, in this verse I can hear You cheering me on. What can I do? *All things!* Who's going to help me? *Christ!* What's He going to do? *Strengthen me!* I praise You for bringing these particular words to me right now. Your Word is so amazing: written thousands of years ago, yet it speaks to us perfectly in our moment of need. What other book is like that? What other god speaks to his people like You do? I know I am going to need this verse today, Lord. Help me to sing it back to You all day long. Amen.

Day 51

THE GOD OF HOSTS

*For, lo, he that formeth the mountains, and
createth the wind, and declareth unto man what
is his thought, that maketh the morning darkness,
and treadeth upon the high places of the earth,
The LORD, The God of hosts, is his name.*

AMOS 4:13 KJV

God, my Father, You formed the mountains and the
wind, the dark of nighttime and the morning's light,
and You lead all the hosts of heaven. You formed my
intricate features inside my mother's womb. Let me
never take for granted Your limitless creativity. Let
me never forget who You truly are.

Day 52

THE CONSTRUCTION SITE

*Being confident of this, that he who began
a good work in you will carry it on to
completion until the day of Christ Jesus.*

PHILIPPIANS 1:6 NIV

God, I am a work in progress. Sometimes I feel like there should be a barrier of construction tape and a hedge of warning signs up around all my rough edges. I am not who I want to be yet, Lord, and I know I'm not who *You* want me to be. Yet (and this is such a huge relief and amazement) You love me anyway. Thank You for Your mercy today and always and for the sure promise that You *are* carrying out Your work in me. Give me fertile soil and a yielding heart. Amen.

Day 53

WORRY LINES

*Don't fret or worry. Instead of worrying, pray.
Let petitions and praises shape your worries into
prayers, letting God know your concerns.*

PHILIPPIANS 4:6 MSG

Dear Lord, I praise You for how You are changing
me. I praise You for how You are teaching me to
place a worry in my open hand and lift it up to You;
if it stays or if it flies away, it belongs to You. I trust
You with my life. Lord, the only worry lines I want
are the creases in the pages of my Bible. I praise You
that *You* are the overcomer; *You* are my resting place;
You are my strength and my fortress. I am so relieved
to lay my worries before You and let them become
prayers. Amen.

Day 54

IF I CAN?!

Jesus said, "If? There are no 'ifs' among believers. Anything can happen."

MARK 9:23 MSG

God, You are so amazing! When You first saved me, I suddenly felt like the world had shifted under me, and anything was possible. Even simple, mundane things such as breathing, eating, and looking up at the sky were made new. The knowledge that You did miracles (and might for me too) made me feel like I was standing on the edge of a new kind of life that was so beautiful and grand I might explode with joy. But it's not just a feeling, Lord. Anything *can* happen. I praise You with open wonder. Amen.

Day 55

MAGNIFYING GLASSES

O magnify the LORD with me,
and let us exalt his name together.

PSALM 34:3 KJV

Remind me, Father God, that I am called to be Your magnifying glass. Shine Your light through me to all the world around me. Move me out of the way so that it's all You that others see. My aim is to exalt Your name in everything I do—in thought, word, and deed. Lead me to other people who are like-minded so that we can truly live lives that worship You and only You.

Day 56

FOOT WASHING

*"By this everyone will know that you are
my disciples, if you love one another."*

JOHN 13:35 NIV

Dear Father, when everything is going well and people are behaving the way I think they should, I find it easy to love. But when the seas are rougher and the sailors are seasick or muttering mutiny, I am appalled at how quickly I become apathetic or mean-spirited. Forgive me, Lord. I want to love like You do. You washed *Judas's* feet! You gently washed the grimy toes of the man who sold You for thirty pieces of silver. What kind of love is that? I could never do that. But Your Spirit, working through my hands, *could*. I praise You for that and so much more.

Day 57

THE ROCK

For the Word that God speaks is alive and full of power. . .it is sharper than any two-edged sword, penetrating to the dividing line of the breath of life (soul) and [the immortal] spirit.

HEBREWS 4:12 AMPC

Dear Father, I have a recurring skeptic in my life. He won't give up or give in, and nothing I say seems to make any difference in his opinion of You or Your Word. He's clinging to nothingness like a limpet on a rock, and I can't pull him off. Lord, I am weary of this fight, and I want to give up. But I know I am here because You put me here with this stubborn mollusk (whom You love). Please give me the strength to keep trying, lovingly and gently, to pry him loose from the big lie he is holding on to. *You* are the only Rock. Amen.

Day 58

OUR REDEEMER

*As for our redeemer, the LORD of hosts
is his name, the Holy One of Israel.*

ISAIAH 47:4 KJV

You are my Redeemer, Lord—You have saved me from all that separated me from You. When I am not holy, You are. When I am trapped in anxiety and despair, You free me. When I see no hope of escape from my present circumstance, You rescue me. When I feel unworthy and stained beyond all hope of saving, You cover me with grace. I worship Your name, Your presence, Your beauty, and Your strength.

Day 59

BABY BLUES

He tends his flock like a shepherd: he gathers the lambs in his arms and carries them close to his heart; he gently leads those that have young.

Isaiah 40:11 niv

Lord, I lift up to You a new mother who is struggling with postpartum depression. With a thirty-six-hour labor, she went from a full-throttle life to a torn body, alien responsibilities, and sleep deprivation. Help her hold on while she heals and adjusts. Surround her with people who will love and support her in practical ways. Be with her husband as he copes with a new baby and a wife who needs him now in ways he never imagined. Bless that little one with health and sleep. Lord, use this time so that they will look back on it and marvel at how You drew them closer to each other and to You. Amen.

Day 60

THE GOD OF OUR SALVATION

Help us, O God of our salvation, for the glory of thy name: and deliver us, and purge away our sins, for thy name's sake.

PSALM 79:9 KJV

When I start to look to other things for my salvation—money, prestige, people, things—remind me, God, that You are the only One who can save me now and keep me safe forever. Remove the temptations from my life that I am so quick to turn to when I'm stressed and insecure. Make me aware of the pitfalls that surround me. Focus my attention on You and Your kingdom.

Day 61

WHO ARE YOUR PHILISTINES?

"The LORD will cause your enemies who rise against you to be defeated before your face; they shall come out against you one way and flee before you seven ways."

DEUTERONOMY 28:7 NKJV

I am not a warrior, Lord. I am a weak woman. You know how many push-ups I can do, how many miles I can run, how long I can go without rest. But I have enemies too. Enemies of anger, self-control, discontent, pride, selfishness, laziness. Strengthen me today for my battles against these foes. You are my high commander, Lord. Strengthen me with Your Spirit so I will be able to resist the enemy of my soul and follow only You. Amen.

Day 62

DON'T TOUCH MY FEET

Jesus answered, "Unless I wash you, you have no part with me."

JOHN 13:8 NIV

Lord, I'm still thinking about foot washing. I can imagine washing someone else's feet, but the idea of having someone—especially You—wash *my* feet makes me squirm. That is appalling grace, like Your offering Yourself up on the cross for us, an act of love so unbelievable that I sometimes don't know what to do with it. How can I say thank You adequately for that? I don't think I ever can. But I will keep trying: thank You, thank You, thank You. Please take away the embarrassment and pride that so often keep me from running to You for the cleansing I desperately need. Amen.

Day 63

GROANING

So too the [Holy] Spirit comes to our aid and bears us up in our weakness; for we do not know what prayer to offer nor how to offer it worthily as we ought, but the Spirit Himself goes to meet our supplication and pleads in our behalf with unspeakable yearnings and groanings too deep for utterance.

ROMANS 8:26 AMPC

Dear Lord, my heart and my mind feel empty right now. I don't know how to pray. I don't know what to pray. I just feel like a great weight is sitting on my chest, and I'm afraid the only thing that's going to come out is a horrible noise filled with tears and tiredness. Oh Father, thank You that You know I am weak and wordless. Thank You for Your Spirit, my Comforter. Speak for me. Amen.

Day 64

HOW'S THE SERVICE?

"For the LORD searches all hearts and understands all the intent of the thoughts. If you seek Him, He will be found by you."

1 CHRONICLES 28:9 NKJV

Dear Lord, I do a lot of things for a lot of people every day. I serve, then serve some more. But, Lord, I am asking You right now to show me my heart. Is my service pleasing to You? Am I serving under obligation, as one who is a slave to sin? Or am I serving with the voluntary spirit of my freedom in Christ? I long to serve without counting the cost. But it's so easy to pray this sort of prayer, Lord, and then go and *do nothing*. Please show me who and how to serve, then help me do it in Jesus' name. Amen.

Day 65

IN TEMPTATION

No test or temptation that comes your way is beyond the course of what others have had to face. All you need to remember is that God will never let you down; he'll never let you be pushed past your limit; he'll always be there to help you come through it.

1 Corinthians 10:13 msg

Dear God, I'm trying to say *no*. Actually, I'm trying to say no to this thing You've asked me to stop doing, and I'm trying to say no to You at the same time. I don't want to be double minded, both asking and doubting; I want Your blessing. So, Lord, help me with my temptation. Other people have struggled with exactly what I am struggling with. It is nothing new, only new to me. But You promise in Your Word that I am strong enough. Help me believe and not doubt. Amen.

Day 66

THE GLORY OF HIS NAME

Give unto the LORD the glory due unto his name:
bring an offering, and come into his courts.

PSALM 96:8 KJV

Lord, fill me with the glory of Your name. May I see
the splendor and light of Your character everywhere
I turn. When I am burdened, show me evidence of
Your love in my daily interactions with others and with
Your creation. I want to always be ready with God-
filled responses to people who ask about my hope.

Day 67

GET OUT OF JAIL FREE

*Whosoever shall call on the name
of the LORD shall be delivered.*

JOEL 2:32 KJV

Father, the world tells me there's no such thing as a free pass. I need to pay my dues, and then someday I may (if I'm lucky) reap the reward. And of course my actions have consequences—the world is quick to remind me of this as well. But, Father, when I am in trouble—when my soul is in captivity—remind me that all I have to do is call Your name. . .and You will set me free.

Day 68

AT YOUR NAIL-TORN FEET

*I have been crucified with Christ and I no longer
live, but Christ lives in me. The life I now live
in the body, I live by faith in the Son of God,
who loved me and gave himself for me.*

GALATIANS 2:20 NIV

Lord, thank You for the story of Ruth. I love the
picture You paint with Boaz, the kinsman-redeemer,
and how he rescued a hungry refugee girl and gave
her the love, prosperity, and hope she was lacking.
And thank You that when You describe Ruth and Boaz,
You are also talking about me and my Savior. Since I
am Your child, that means Jesus is my kinsman-
redeemer too. I throw myself at Your feet, Jesus. Cover
me with Your garment of grace. Live in me. Amen.

Day 69

MAJESTY AND STRENGTH

And he shall stand and feed in the strength of the
LORD, in the majesty of the name of the LORD his God.

MICAH 5:4 KJV

Lord, I admit that the stress of life and the burdens of
this world often leave me feeling weak and powerless.
But Your name is majesty and strength. Your name
is higher, more powerful, and far more excellent
than anything this world has to offer me. All I need
to do is tap into the power of Your name, and You
promise to sustain me. I can do all things through You
because You give me strength!

THE HOLLOW

Keep me as the apple of your eye;
hide me in the shadow of your wings.

PSALM 17:8 NIV

Jesus, when I think about You making Your home in my heart, I imagine a little creature padding a tree hollow with leaves and dry grasses and turning in a tight, furry circle and falling asleep. The tree is strong—an oak, perhaps, or a towering hemlock—and will stand unbowed through the winter storms. I am that furry creature, Lord: a well-beloved, dear thing. And You are the tree. It is not so much that You live in *me*, but that I live in *You*. Thank You for letting me burrow into Your deep, safe, warm heart, Lord, and remain. Amen.

Day 11

JESUS IN MY HEART

And I will ask the Father, and He will give you another Comforter (Counselor, Helper, Intercessor, Advocate, Strengthener, and Standby), that He may remain with you forever.

JOHN 14:16 AMPC

Lord, sometimes I think of how the disciples must have felt after they watched You ascend into heaven: bereft, terrified, rootless. You had been everything to them, and suddenly You were gone. *What now?* they must have wondered. But forty days later, You were back. Not just for a visit but to *live* in them forever. Lord, You promise never to leave me or forsake me, and because of the great gift of Your Spirit, I know I am not alone. Thank You that You have made Your home in my heart. Amen.

Day 72

SINGING GOD'S NAME

I will praise the name of God with a song,
and will magnify him with thanksgiving.

PSALM 69:30 KJV

God, fill me with Your song today. Orchestrate within my heart a melody that is truly a joyful noise, one that will bring gladness to Your heart. Give me words of praise to You and words of encouragement for others. Fill my song with Your peace and Your beauty. Help me to live out that song every moment, regardless of my circumstances. May I hallow Your name with singing.

Day 13

IN QUIETNESS

*For thus saith the Lord GOD, the Holy One of
Israel; in returning and rest shall ye be saved; in
quietness and in confidence shall be your strength.*

ISAIAH 30:15 KJV

Lord, sometimes it feels like I never sit down. There
are always so many things to do: people to manage,
dishes to wash, bills to pay, groceries to buy, toilets
to fix, emails to answer. The noise and busyness of
my life seem unending. But I know You call me to
come away, just as Jesus did, and come to You in
quietness and rest. Not just because You desire it,
but because that quietness and rest in Your presence
is the source of my strength. Thank You for longing
to protect my heart in this crazy, merry-go-round
world. Amen.

Day 74

A GOD OF JUSTICE

For I the Lord love judgment, I hate robbery.

Isaiah 61:8 kjv

If I hallow Your name, God, then I need to remember just who You really are: a God of justice. Remind me that You have called me to show the same justice in everything I do. Thank You for being the perfect balance of justice and mercy, of fairness and love. Try as I might, I cannot strike that balance in my life without Your help. Teach me to love justice and strive for justice every day.

Day 75

THE AMEN INCARNATE

"These are the words of the Amen, the faithful and true witness, the ruler of God's creation."

REVELATION 3:14 NIV

Dear Father, so many portraits paint Jesus as a soft, almost wilting, white man. But I bet You weren't: I bet You were dark and as hard as nails. I bet Your feet were cut and Your hands were scarred even before the cross. Yet You are also the image of the invisible God. You are the Amen, the *so be it*. There is an equation here, the solution of which is just beyond my grasp. Jesus equals the image of God equals Amen equals *so be it*. I am so glad You are not easy to figure out. I am so thankful that You offer mystery and puzzles and food for thought that will satisfy my soul for eternity. Amen.

Day 16

FACE TO GRACE

And He said to me, "My grace is sufficient for you, for My strength is made perfect in weakness." Therefore most gladly I will rather boast in my infirmities, that the power of Christ may rest upon me.

2 Corinthians 12:9 nkjv

Father, my friend who loves You is dying. Her body is a minefield of cancer; the doctor says she has just weeks to live. Just a few weeks until she sees You face-to-face! But I praise You, Lord, in the midst of my tears because the power of Christ is so visibly resting on her right now, as she stands with her face touching the veil, seeing shadows of the next life. Only You can do this: give a woman, wasting away and saying goodbye to her young family, a joy and strength that evangelizes *others*. Even if You don't heal her, she is giving You all the glory. And I am seeing Your wonders. Amen.

Day 11

CALLED BY HIS NAME

Thy words were found, and I did eat them; and thy word was unto me the joy and rejoicing of mine heart: for I am called by thy name, O L ORD God of hosts.

JEREMIAH 15:16 KJV

Oh God, not only have You adopted me as Your child, but now You say I also have Your name as my own. You pursued me, You purchased me, You accepted me, You love me. Although I don't deserve the honor of being called Yours, I am so happy to accept the gift. Help me strive to be worthy of it.

Day 78

STRENGTH IN JOY

Nehemiah said, "Go and enjoy choice food and sweet drinks, and send some to those who have nothing prepared. This day is holy to our Lord. Do not grieve, for the joy of the LORD is your strength."

NEHEMIAH 8:10 NIV

So often, Lord, I walk around with a glum face, as if being a child of the only living God weren't something to cheer about every moment of every day. I complain about how much work I have to do, how little I am appreciated, how relentlessly hard life seems sometimes. But You tell me in this verse to do these things: eat something yummy (thanks, Lord!), drink, share with others. Since Jesus came to earth, every day is a celebration. And Your festival-joy is the strength I need to keep on. Amen.

Day 79

SO BE IT

The effective, fervent prayer of a
righteous man avails much.

JAMES 5:16 NKJV

Dearest Lord, I know what I want, but I can't see the future. I know what I think would be best for me and the people around me, but I don't have Your eyes. So I pray, but I hold my prayers lightly. Are they Your will? Am I praying rightly? Show me, Lord. When I pray *Amen*, I think what I really mean is *Your will be done.* And it's a conundrum: I know Your will *will* be done, yet You ask me to pray also. Why, Lord? I long to obey with knowledge, but for now I will simply obey. And wait on You. Amen.

Day 80

EATING GOD'S HOLINESS

That we might be partakers of his holiness.

HEBREWS 12:10 KJV

Father, I honor Your name by taking my fill each day of Your holiness. Make Your Spirit alive and active in my heart today. Remind me to always seek You through prayer, meditation on Your Word, and simply being still in Your presence. And when I get "too busy" to take the time to spend with You, please invite me back into Your presence. I can't handle life on my own. . .nor do I want to.

Day 81

IN A DRY TIME

*On the last and greatest day of the festival, Jesus
stood and said in a loud voice, "Let anyone
who is thirsty come to me and drink. Whoever
believes in me, as Scripture has said, rivers of
living water will flow from within them."*

JOHN 7:37–38 NIV

Dear Father, I want to pray because You are beautiful
and I love You, but the words will not come. I am dry
and thirsty. But You are the living water, Jesus. You
tell me in Your Word that if I come to You, streams of
living water will flow from within me. Thank You for
that promise. I am assured that this dry time will not
last if I am faithful to come to You for refreshing. I am
waiting on You.

Day 82

LIGHT

God is light, and in him is no darkness at all.

1 John 1:5 kjv

Father God, Your name is light. You have no darkness in Your character. Your brilliance is dazzling—brighter than the brightest star and more beautiful than the most awe-inspiring celestial display. You are a hope-filled promise of never-ending illumination. Please shine on me—and shine *through* me so that others may see the darkness of this world flee before Your light.

Day 83

THE ROCK

*The LORD is my rock, and my fortress, and
my deliverer; my God, my strength, in whom
I will trust; my buckler, and the horn of
my salvation, and my high tower.*

PSALM 18:2 KJV

So many names You have, Lord: Rock, Fortress,
Deliverer, Buckler, Horn of Salvation, High Tower.
All of them tell me that I can trust You absolutely.
All of them tell me You are in control, that You will
shield me from danger, that I shouldn't be afraid,
that I am safe in Your mighty hand. You will never
let me down.

Day 84

DINNER AT JESUS' HOUSE

"Behold, I stand at the door and knock; if anyone hears My voice and opens the door, I will come in to him and will dine with him, and he with Me."

REVELATION 3:20 NASB

Dear Father, I am so blessed that You continue to mold and shape me into the likeness of Your Son. Your Word says that Jesus didn't really have a home of His own. His home was wherever on the road He happened to be when night fell. But today, it hit me that my home, this walled place with bedrooms and tables and bathrooms, really is Jesus' home too. I ask Your blessing, Lord, as I seek to understand what that kind of a house is like. I ask for Your grace and power to be real in our lives, *here*. Amen.

Day 85

TRUTH

Lead me in thy truth, and teach me: for thou art the God of my salvation; on thee do I wait all the day.

PSALM 25:5 KJV

Your Son said He was the Way, the Truth, and the Life. Father, may I always walk in Your truth, the truth of Jesus. Teach me patience as I wait for You to move, to act in my life, as I wait for Your return. Waiting is not an easy thing to do, God. Please give me the strength to trust in the hope of my salvation in You. Your truth means everything to me.

Day 86

OUT OF SIGHT

*And when he was demanded of the Pharisees,
when the kingdom of God should come,
he answered them and said, The kingdom
of God cometh not with observation.*

LUKE 17:20 KJV

Father, I can't always see the reality of Your kingdom in the world around me. Give me eyes of faith. Show me the people who are working for Your goals, and give me opportunity to serve alongside them. Allow me to bring Your kingdom to the people and places around me that need You most.

Day 87

UNWRAPPING JESUS

But the gift is not like the trespass. For if the many died by the trespass of the one man, how much more did God's grace and the gift that came by the grace of the one man, Jesus Christ, overflow to the many!

ROMANS 5:15 NIV

It's dark, Lord, before the dawn on Your birthday. I can imagine what this dawn was like two thousand years ago. Mary and Joseph had been up all night, laboring on the straw, exhausted and filthy and terrified. Were You born at sunrise? We celebrate Your birth now with tinsel, decorated trees, and toys. But You came with blood and tears and terror. My children will be awake soon, Lord, and I want this day to be different than it usually is. Help me show them how the gift of Jesus outshines and outlasts all the glitter. Amen.

Day 88

DETOURS ON THE WAY TO AMEN

Strengthened with all might, according to his glorious power, unto all patience and longsuffering with joyfulness.

<small>COLOSSIANS 1:11 KJV</small>

Father, I never seem to be able to get to *Amen* in one go. With people around me all day long (and no prayer closets with locks), quiet times are more like dull-roar times. But when I study Your Word, Lord, I am often so surprised: Jesus going off alone into the wilderness to pray, then being followed by the disciples who, like little children, can't seem to get enough of Him. They interrupt His prayers with questions and comments, and He never once says, "Go away, can't you see I'm praying?" Interrupt me, Lord, and conform my character into that of Your precious Son. Amen.

Day 89

GOOD NEWS

He went throughout every city and village, preaching and shewing the glad tidings of the kingdom of God.

LUKE 8:1 KJV

Make me Your ambassador, Lord, carrying the good news of Your kingdom to everyone I meet today. Give me new opportunities and new relationships that I might not normally notice, so I can reach more hearts for You. Help me to see these individuals through Your eyes, as loved children of God created in Your image. Give me the right words to say, and open their ears so they can truly understand the glad tidings of Your kingdom.

Day 90

TRAIL SIGNS

Your ears shall hear a word behind you, saying,
"This is the way, walk in it," whenever you turn
to the right hand or whenever you turn to the left.

ISAIAH 30:21 NKJV

Dear God, I just want to thank You for speaking to me through another believer and keeping me from sin. Lord, You know how I longed to send that email and share something I shouldn't have. I was about to gossip, and I'm sorry. I'm so glad You sent someone to stand behind me and read over my shoulder and gently tell me not to hit SEND. Amen.

Day 91

RIGHTEOUSNESS, PEACE, AND JOY

*For the kingdom of God is not meat
and drink; but righteousness, and
peace, and joy in the Holy Ghost.*

ROMANS 14:17 KJV

Remind me, Father (because I forget so easily), that Your kingdom is not built on the things of this world. The truth is that Your kingdom flies in the face of the things of the world. Righteousness, peace, and joy are heavenly attributes that we humans have a difficult time living out without Your Spirit to change our hearts. May I not depend on external reality for my satisfaction but instead dwell always in Your realm of peace and joy.

Day 92

THE SOWER

*And he said, So is the kingdom of God, as if
a man should cast seed into the ground.*

MARK 4:26 KJV

God, what does this mean: Your kingdom is like a man
casting seed on the ground? Does this mean I can find
Your kingdom everywhere, scattered throughout our
world by Your generous hand? Give me new eyes to
see Your kingdom all around me, especially in places
I wouldn't expect to see You. Father, thank You for
Your generosity. Thank You that You do not ever
withhold Yourself but are always giving.

Day 93

FASTER, DONKEY?

"Be still, and know that I am God."

PSALM 46:10 NIV

Jesus, did You ever hurry? Were You ever in a rush as You walked from Cana to Capernaum? Were You ever late for dinner with Mary and Martha? Did You ever kick Your heels into the donkey's side so it would trot just a bit faster? I don't think so, Lord. Your Word shows You differently: wherever You were was exactly where You wanted to be at that moment, even on the cross. I long to be like that. Please help me slow down and savor this life You have blessed me with: the small moments of glory, quiet words with a friend, even the daily struggles that are conforming me to Your image. I am *here*, and so are You. Amen.

Day 94

JESUS LIVES HERE

*"Martha, Martha," the Lord answered, "you
are worried and upset about many things,
but few things are needed—or indeed only
one. Mary has chosen what is better, and
it will not be taken away from her."*

LUKE 10:41–42 NIV

Dear Jesus, You loved visiting Mary and Martha. Their
house must have been a place of comfort, rest, and
welcome for You. I wish I could sit at Your feet like
Mary did, but then I realize that when I open Your
Word, I am. Make my heart welcoming too, Lord,
not a place of sharp corners, cobwebs, and hidden
sins. Throw open the windows, and let Your light
shine in and out. Amen.

Day 95

A MUSTARD SEED

The kingdom of God. . .is like a grain of mustard seed, which, when it is sown in the earth, is less than all the seeds that be in the earth.

MARK 4:30–31 KJV

Lord, in order for Your kingdom to grow and expand, please plant a seed of faith in my heart. Make my heart a fertile place for that faith to grow so that my work in Your kingdom will be fruitful. Embolden Your Spirit in me so that I might contribute greatly to Your plans—not for my glory but for Yours alone, Father.

BEFORE THE DOORBELL RINGS

All the days of the afflicted are evil, but he who is of a merry heart has a continual feast.

PROVERBS 15:15 NKJV

Dear Lord, I so wanted to have some quiet moments with You this morning. But the baby woke up early, the plumber called to say he's on his way, and the day is rushing at me down the tracks like a train. But I am going to choose joy today, Lord. I am going to choose to take what You give with open arms. I can pray where I stand, as I walk and talk; I can meditate on Your Word in any and every situation. And maybe I can get up earlier tomorrow! Amen.

Day 97

LIKE A CHILD

Verily I say unto you, Whosoever shall not receive the kingdom of God as a little child, he shall not enter therein.

MARK 10:15 KJV

Give me a child's heart, Lord. Create in me the simple and heartfelt belief that You celebrate and cherish in Your children. Let me experience the wonder of Your love and gift of grace. Help me to share with others, with childlike exuberance, the hope I have in You. Let me set aside grown-up worries and live a joyful life so that I can enter Your kingdom.

Day 98

MORE THAN JUST TALK

For the kingdom of God is not in word, but in power.

<small>1 Corinthians 4:20 kjv</small>

God, sometimes I talk a good game, but my heart and actions don't carry it through. Remind me that Your kingdom is active and powerful. It's not just a bunch of talk. It's real and it's here on earth now. You ask me to help build Your kingdom; show me new ways to serve. Give me a passion for Your kingdom on earth—and for Your heavenly kingdom as well.

Day 99

AFTER THE AMEN

"Who among all these does not know that the hand of the LORD has done this, in whose hand is the life of every living thing, and the breath of all mankind?"

JOB 12:9–10 NASB

So, Father, where do I go from here? How do I live once I get up off my knees? I like quick fixes, amazing tricks that promise to solve problems in three easy steps. But I know You are not like that. Sometimes the miraculous intervenes, but more often the Christian life is—as I heard one author put it—a long obedience in the same direction. Maybe what You've shown me most clearly, Lord, is not to wait for everything to be "perfect" before I try to follow You more faithfully. Help me to—standing, sitting, lying down, or running—*live* as though I'm on my knees. Amen.

Day 100

WHO HOLDS THE REINS?

All the ways of a man are pure in his own eyes, but the LORD weighs the spirits. Commit your works to the LORD, and your thoughts will be established.

PROVERBS 16:2–3 NKJV

Dear Father, I spend so much time trying to control others. Futilely. I feel my anxiety mounting, and I know that is not what You want. I can only control my own heart, Lord, and that is only because of Your grace and the gift of Your Spirit. I can't be the "holy spirit" of anyone else's heart. That is Your job. Please help me let go of my agenda and instead lift others up to You. Work on and through *me*, Lord, so they would be drawn closer to You. Amen.

Day 101

BLESSED POVERTY

Blessed be ye poor: for yours is the kingdom of God.
LUKE 6:20 KJV

Lord, make me willing to be poor in this world so that I can be rich in Your kingdom. Give me a spirit of generosity, even giving beyond my comfort level so that I must sacrifice my feelings of security. The things of earth are not the important things, God. I know You will take care of me, and You promise me an even greater reward in heaven.

Day 102

FALLING INTO LIGHT

I bow my knees before the Father. . .that He would
grant you, according to the riches of His glory, to
be strengthened with power through His Spirit.

EPHESIANS 3:14, 16 NASB

Dear Lord, again I thank You for Your precious Word.
Thank You for the prayer You gave us in Ephesians 3 and
how it has enriched my understanding of You. When
I fall to my knees, You will strengthen me. I fall, Lord,
because I am weak and because You are great, and then
in falling, miraculously, Your strength becomes mine.
You dwell in me. Your boundless love bears fruit in me:
enough both to keep and to give away. I—weak, broken,
sin scarred, blind—am strong, whole, pure, clear-eyed,
and filled with the fullness of God. Praise God!

Day 103

DEAD AND GONE

Jesus said unto him, Let the dead bury their dead:
but go thou and preach the kingdom of God.

LUKE 9:60 KJV

God, help me to let go of the past and look instead to
Your future. I know that You hold my past, present,
and future in Your hand. I give You all three, and I ask
You to be my Savior that covers my past sin, lead me in
Your will in my present circumstance, and be with me
as I move into Your future. May I not be preoccupied
with that which is dead and gone; fill my thoughts and
conversation with the reality of Your kingdom in the
here and now.

Day 104

CLEAN HOUSE

*So that He might sanctify her, having cleansed
her by the washing of water with the Word.*

Ephesians 5:26 ampc

Dear God, my house is so messy. I just don't seem to have time to get the cobwebs off the ceiling or clean the drips off the fronts of the cabinets or scrub the smudges off the walls around the light switches. Please help me be content with imperfection, because sometimes it seems like I can either clean or read Your Word but not both. And I know it is far more important to wash the house of my soul with Your living water. Amen.

Day 105

HEALING

And heal the sick that are therein, and say unto them, The kingdom of God is come nigh unto you.

LUKE 10:9 KJV

Your kingdom, Lord, brings healing to those who are sick in spirit, mind, or body. Enable me to carry Your healing to those around me. Keep me accountable; remind me to not just *say* that I will pray for others who are sick but to earnestly and intentionally come to You on their behalf. Help me to see the healing miracles You supply every moment of every day. And remind me to point others to Your goodness in those situations.

THE LORD IS IN THE HOUSE

But when the kindness and love of God our Savior appeared, he saved us, not because of righteous things we had done, but because of his mercy. He saved us through the washing of rebirth and renewal by the Holy Spirit.

TITUS 3:4–5 NIV

Dear Jesus, sometimes I imagine that You are in my house, sitting and watching our activities from the couch like a well-beloved guest. Thank You, Lord, that You care enough to come and stay. God's perfection is blinding and searing and annihilating, and if not for You, Jesus, we would die of it. You are holy (and wholly different) but still a man. I praise You, Jesus, for the sweetness of Your fellowship and the surprising ways You teach us to love. Amen.

Day 101

SANCTIFICATION

For this is the will of God, even your sanctification.

1 THESSALONIANS 4:3 KJV

God, Ruler of my life, You want me to be sanctified— wholly, utterly given to You. I surrender myself to Your will. I give You my heart, my family relationships, my friend relationships, my career, my ministry, my hobbies, my health. Gently prod me along to continue to surrender every area of my life to You—especially the ones that I try so desperately to take back and control on my own. Amen.

Day 108

THANKS

In every thing give thanks: for this is the will of God.
1 Thessalonians 5:18 KJV

King of the universe, I give You thanks for all You have given me every moment of the day. Thanks for the health You've granted that allows me to wake up feeling alert and refreshed. Thank You for the food that nourishes my body to do Your work. Thank You for the clothes You have provided to keep me warm. Thank You for work to do so I may glorify You. Continue to fill my heart with gratitude so that I may do Your will in the world.

Day 109

A LONG WAY OFF

*"When he was still a great way off, his father
saw him and had compassion, and ran
and fell on his neck and kissed him."*

LUKE 15:20 NKJV

Dear Lord, I can't even remember where I was three months ago when I began this journey to draw closer to You. I was in a different place; *I* was different. Just like the prodigal son, I am still a long way off. I am far from where You want me and far, even, from where I want to be—and I'm usually pretty easy on myself. But I praise You for drawing me closer. I praise You for how Your Word has soothed the rough, bitter edges of my heart and washed away years of silt and sin. Please help me go forward from here, drinking deeper and believing harder that He who promises is faithful. Amen.

Day 110

WORDS, WORDS, WORDS

*As newborn babes, desire the pure milk of the
word, that you may grow thereby, if indeed
you have tasted that the Lord is gracious.*

1 PETER 2:2–3 NKJV

Dear Father, my life is so full of words: books, TV, movies, neighbors, family, friends, letters, email, advertisements, radio. I am bombarded by them (and bombard others with mine) all day long, and I wonder how many of them really glorify You. And that *is* my desire, Lord: to glorify You. Please help me filter from the filth and froth what is pure and gracious. Help me desire truly to drink only Your pure milk so that it would flow out through me. Amen.

Day 111

DELIGHT

I delight to do thy will, O my God.

PSALM 40:8 KJV

Thank You, God, that Your will is not one of sadness and gloom. I am grateful that You are not a God that relishes seeing Your children suffer. In fact, You take great pleasure in giving good gifts to me! What a joy to know that You think of me in that way! As I learn to live always within Your kingdom, I am delighted to be able to give back in some small way as I serve You and others.

Day 112

TIME FOR HEALING

*He heals the brokenhearted and
binds up their wounds.*

PSALM 147:3 NASB

Dear Lord, I find myself obsessing over certain people who upset me, like I'm picking at scabs. I think about how they have wounded me, and those wounds become deeper and sadder. Lord, when I do this, I am pushing Jesus out. I am not letting Him come into these situations and offer His gifts of forgiveness and healing. Please forgive me for relishing my wounds more than Your healing. Help me pray *for* people instead of muttering against them. I want to know You, Lord, and the power of Your resurrection, even in my small hurts. Amen.

Day 113

FOREVER

And the world passeth away, and the lust thereof:
but he that doeth the will of God abideth for ever.

1 John 2:17 kjv

The things of this world never last. I don't know why I get excited about acquiring material things. The anticipation is better than the real thing, which always ends in disappointment. Even my cravings for this world's things come and go. Thank You, Lord God, that Your kingdom is permanent, and I will dwell there forever. Give me a passion for eternity with You—payoff that absolutely will not disappoint!

Day 114

FIRST THINGS FIRST

*But seek ye first the kingdom of God,
and his righteousness; and all these
things shall be added unto you.*

MATTHEW 6:33 KJV

You understand, Lord, that I have bills to pay, deadlines to meet, a house to clean, a family to care for. These things are important, but they don't have ultimate importance. Remind me always to seek Your kingdom ahead of all these things. Give me a life of balance that is faithfully committed to Your call. Help me to trust that You will take care of (and bless) the details of my life.

Day 115

JOY SCHOOL

"Come to Me, all who are weary and heavy-laden, and I will give you rest. Take My yoke upon you and learn from Me, for I am gentle and humble in heart, and YOU WILL FIND REST FOR YOUR SOULS."

MATTHEW 11:28–29 NASB

Joy is not my native language, Lord. I am more fluent in complaint, agitation, and bitterness. But this tongue of lead is heavy and wearying. I long to speak like the angels at the dawn of creation when they all shouted for joy! This is what I would say: "You are good! You are holy! You are God!" Those are the words that people are dying to hear. Thank You that I am made in Your image so I can grow and change. I am not an animal, bound by nature; I can learn another tongue. Amen.

AMAZING FORGIVENESS

In Him we have redemption through His blood, the forgiveness of sins, according to the riches of His grace.

EPHESIANS 1:7 NKJV

Lord, I come into Your presence, thanking You for forgiveness. In a culture where many experience clinical depression because of guilt, I can know my past is redeemed because of Christ's sacrifice for me. Your forgiveness is so amazing. Although I don't deserve it, You pour it out freely and lovingly. Because You have seen fit to pardon me, I bless Your name today.

Day 117

PATIENCE

*For ye have need of patience, that, after ye have
done the will of God, ye might receive the promise.*

HEBREWS 10:36 KJV

King of my heart, I want to do Your will. You know
that sometimes, though, I grow impatient and filled
with doubt. I am distracted by the temptations of
the world—money, relationships, power, prestige—
that look like answers to my problems. In my heart
of hearts, I know they will only lead to ruin. Help
me to keep going, relying on You. I know You always
keep Your promises.

Day 118

HEART TRANSPLANT

Therefore, if anyone is in Christ, the new creation has come: The old has gone, the new is here!

2 CORINTHIANS 5:17 NIV

Dear Father, You have blessed me with a healthy body, and I praise You for it. I have aches and pains and odd cramps and mysterious rumblings, but I've never had any broken bones, stitches, or spent the night in a hospital for anything except tonsils and childbirth! Thank You, Father. Many are not so blessed. But we all have hidden wounds, Father, wounds that bleed out onto other people. You know what mine are even better than I do. You are the great Healer, Lord. You heal with a touch, with a word. You heal simply with Your presence. Show me my hurts, Lord, and heal them. Amen.

Day 119

ENOUGH

God is able to make all grace abound toward you; that ye, always having all sufficiency in all things, may abound to every good work.

2 CORINTHIANS 9:8 KJV

You make me sufficient, Lord—You give me enough of everything I need—to carry out Your will. Truth be told, You often supply *much more* than I need. These blessings are wonderful surprises that I don't want to take for granted. Show me ways that I can share Your blessings with others. You are a good giver, Lord. Thank You.

PROVISIONS FROM GOD

*You open Your hand and satisfy
the desire of every living thing.*

PSALM 145:16 NKJV

God, there is no creature on earth You do not see or provide for. I'm bringing praise to You right now for the daily things You supply for me. It is through Your goodness that I have food to eat, clothes to wear, and water to drink. Help me to always be thankful for what I have and to not emulate the wandering Israelites who, focusing on lack, preferred to complain. Your power is awesome; thank You for generously supplying my needs and wants each and every day.

Day 121

REST

"For in six days the LORD made the heavens and the earth, the sea, and all that is in them, and rested the seventh day. Therefore the LORD blessed the Sabbath day and hallowed it."

EXODUS 20:11 NKJV

Dear Lord, it is Sunday today. Every day is Your day, but You set aside this one specifically for us to rest and worship You. Rest does not come easily to me, Lord. I plan and work and *do*. Resting seems somehow self-indulgent and lazy. But Your thoughts toward me are numerous and higher than mine. I don't know what I need, but You do. Plans will be made today; messes will be made. Help me decide what honors Your commandment best in each situation: doing or waiting. Help me make my home and heart places of rest and worship. Show me what that means to You. Amen.

Day 122

GOD'S RICHES

*My God shall supply all your need according
to his riches in glory by Christ Jesus.*

PHILIPPIANS 4:19 KJV

Why should I ever doubt Your ability to give me what
I need, heavenly Father, when You have such riches?
Your bounty is unfathomable, and You want to share
it with me! How humbling! Help me to remember
that everything I call "mine" is actually Yours. Forgive
me when my heart is hard and unwilling to accept
Your riches in glory. Help me to be open to Your
Spirit as He moves in my heart.

Day 123

PRAY FOR ME

The LORD thunders at the head of his army;
his forces are beyond number, and mighty
is the army that obeys his command.

JOEL 2:11 NIV

Dear Lord, how many times have I told someone I
would pray for them, then never did? Those were lies,
Lord. Forgetting to pray is like leaving a wounded
fellow soldier behind on the battlefield. Forgive me.
But I need You to help me remember, Lord, for my
mind is small and harried and easily overrun. I trust
You to be my general and bring them to mind when
the fighting is fiercest and the need is greatest. Help
me keep my heart and ears open to Your commands.
Amen.

Day 124

NO WANTS

The LORD is my shepherd; I shall not want.
PSALM 23:1 KJV

Since You are looking out for me—guarding and guiding me—I have everything I need. You are the Good Shepherd who supplies everything to me, Your sheep. Remind me every day that, as a sheep, I cannot see the bigger picture—the dangers over the hill or the blessings that are mine to find. Help me more fully trust the Shepherd and His plans for me. Give me a heart of gratitude and a spirit that relinquishes control. Thank You, Lord.

Day 125

NONE LIKE YOU

"No one is holy like the LORD, for there is none besides You, nor is there any rock like our God."

1 SAMUEL 2:2 NKJV

God, when I consider my own inadequacies, I am amazed at Your perfectness. You are truth and justice, holiness and integrity. There is none like You. You are the one and only true God. Other deities disappoint their followers; other idols fail. But You never do. Because You are perfect holiness, all Your other attributes are only good. There is no selfishness, vengefulness, or deceitfulness in You, Lord. Thus, I can trust You completely and revel in Your light unafraid. Amen.

Day 126

SEED AND BREAD

Now he that ministereth seed to the sower both minister bread for your food, and multiply your seed sown, and increase the fruits of your righteousness.

2 CORINTHIANS 9:10 KJV

God, You aren't just a sower or a harvester; You're a true farmer. First You plant the seed; then You water it and nurture it, giving me the food and encouragement I need to grow in You. You work tirelessly to reap a bountiful harvest when my heart is full of fertile soil. I want to return the harvest to You, bearing beautiful fruits of righteousness. Keep working on me, farmer God—I am willing.

RIGHT THERE WITH ME

*I will praise the LORD, who counsels me;
even at night my heart instructs me.*

PSALM 16:7 NIV

Dear God, how many times have I gone to sleep with a problem weighing on my mind and woken up in the morning with a solution that seemed to appear out of nowhere as I slept. I realize now that those miraculous solutions come from You. Thank You, Lord, for counseling me in the night, for instructing me even when I am not aware of it. It comforts me to know that You are so intimately concerned with me and that even when I don't see Your hand or hear Your voice, You are right there with me. Amen.

Day 128

LIKE BIRDS

Consider the ravens: for they neither sow nor reap; which neither have storehouse nor barn; and God feedeth them: how much more are ye better than the fowls?

LUKE 12:24 KJV

Lord, if You keep track of the lives of birds, then I know I can trust You to watch over my own life. May I rest in the knowledge that You are always looking after me. I know I am worth much more to You than a bird. And even though I know I don't deserve it, I thank You for Your unconditional love.

Day 129

PRIORITIES

Therefore I say unto you, Take no thought for your life, what ye shall eat, or what ye shall drink; nor yet for your body, what ye shall put on. Is not the life more than meat, and the body than raiment?

MATTHEW 6:25 KJV

When I start to worry over little things, help me to keep my priorities in order, Father God. Give me grace not to make mountains out of molehills. Time and time again, You have proven that You are faithful to take care of me, so what right do I have to worry? Keep my heart steadfast and my footing secure in the knowledge that You hold me in Your hand.

Day 130

ROOTED

A man is not established by wickedness,
but the root of the righteous cannot be moved.

PROVERBS 12:3 NKJV

Lord, please forgive me. This has been a hard time, and I have been entertaining doubts of all sorts. I am just realizing, as I sit here in the quiet with You, that I was under attack and I parleyed with the enemy. I now see how the attack went: first pride, then a judging spirit, then self-doubt, then bitterness, then despair, then an existential doubt of the foulest sort. *Do You love me? Are You really there?* I long to grow deep, Lord. I am tired of being torn out by the roots over and over. Give me the diligence I am lacking to grow deep in You, down through streams of living water to the solid Rock. Amen.

Day 131

THE INSPIRATIONAL WORD

*All Scripture is God-breathed and is
useful for teaching, rebuking, correcting
and training in righteousness.*

2 TIMOTHY 3:16 NIV

Lord, Your Word thrills me, convicts me, comforts me,
and strengthens me. I am so thankful that You gave us
the Bible. Thank You for inspiring the prophets of old
as they penned Your truth. Thank You for protecting
the scripture through centuries of skepticism and
persecution. Thank You for giving me the blessing of
this treasure, for allowing me to hold it in my hand.
When I am hungry, Your Word feeds me; when I am
fearful, it assures me; when I am uncertain, it guides
me. Your Book is the light upon my path. Without it,
I would be lost. Amen.

Day 132

DEEPER

They have bowed down and fallen;
but we have risen and stand upright.

PSALM 20:8 NKJV

How much is enough, Lord? How deep is deep enough? I read once that the deepest tree roots ever recorded went down well over one hundred feet. I want to be that deep in You. I want the energy of my growth to go downward, not to attractive but weak side branches that just sap my strength. Show me what I need to prune from my life, Lord. Make me willing to clip and snip and shape. Lord, I'm sure Paul's good looks were marred by the beatings, imprisonment, snakebites, and shipwrecks he endured for Your sake, but how firmly he stood! Help me value a firm, rooted faith more than pretty flowers and a pleasing appearance. Amen.

Day 133

PRAYER AND THANKSGIVING

*Be careful for nothing; but in every thing by
prayer and supplication with thanksgiving let
your requests be made known unto God.*

PHILIPPIANS 4:6 KJV

Even while I'm asking You for something, Lord, I can
already thank You. I know You hear my prayers and
will answer with "Yes," "No," or "Wait." Thank You
for often taking care of my needs even before I ask.
What a comfort it is that You already know what I
need. I can trust You absolutely to answer me in the
best way and according to Your purpose.

DIVERSE GIFTS

There are different kinds of gifts, but the same Spirit.

1 Corinthians 12:4 niv

Dear God, today the fellowship of other believers ministered to me. There are times when I get frustrated with the church—it has its challenges. But so does a human body. And yet when each bodily organ serves the function for which it was made, there is life, energy, and passion. Help me remember, Lord, that You made my spiritual brothers and sisters with diverse gifts; help me work with them, not against them. Thank You for reminding me again today this family of God is one of Your treasures, a blessing from Your hand—and heart. Amen.

GOD'S EARS

And if we know that he hear us, whatsoever
we ask, we know that we have the
petitions that we desired of him.

1 JOHN 5:15 KJV

Thank You, God, that You are always listening to me. You never ignore my prayers, no matter how silly or insignificant I think my words might be. It's a mystery how You can possibly hear the requests of all of mankind at the same time, but You do! And each moment of communication is important to You. Thank You for being a God with always-listening ears.

Day 136

STRONGER

*And we know that all things work together
for good to them that love God, to them who
are the called according to his purpose.*

ROMANS 8:28 KJV

Lord, You know this is a difficult season in my life. When I was younger, You staked and sheltered me like a precious sapling, but now I am faced with stresses that I never imagined before. Sickness, grief, aging, loss, hardship. But yet I stand. I am amazed at the strength You are giving me daily. Lord, I know myself, and I *know* this is all from You. All these things You are using for Your glory. I know I won't look back from heaven at the events of my life and say anything other than *hallelujah*. I am saying it now. *Hallelujah. Hallelujah.*

Day 137

PROMISES

*Whatsoever we ask, we receive of him, because
we keep his commandments, and do those
things that are pleasing in his sight.*

1 JOHN 3:22 KJV

Help me to keep Your commandments and always
live in a way that pleases You, my Lord. I know Your
commandments are not meant to be a burden to me
but to keep me safe from harm, from temptations, and
to allow me to live in the freedom of Your love. Forgive
me for the times I feel like Your laws are constraining
to me.

Day 138

TO EVERY GENERATION

Your faithfulness endures to all generations.

PSALM 119:90 NKJV

Jehovah God, I come just now to revel in Your faithfulness. From generations past to this very minute, multitudes have testified that You always come through. Yet there have been times in my life when I thought You had overlooked me, that You weren't aware of my needs, that You didn't hear my prayers. But my doubts proved false, and Your record is untarnished. You didn't promise that I would always understand Your ways, but You did promise Your presence and love in every circumstance. And I can testify it's true. I love You, Lord. Amen.

Day 139

PERSISTENCE!

Ask, and it shall be given you; seek, and ye shall find; knock, and it shall be opened unto you.

MATTHEW 7:7 KJV

May I trust You enough, Lord, to ask You for what I need—and then to keep asking, seeking, and knocking until You answer. Help me not to grow weary in coming to You in prayer. I know that You will keep Your promises—that You hear me and are working in the details of my life. When I am praying for others, keep me committed to taking them to You.

BRIGHTER

The entrance and unfolding of Your words
give light; their unfolding gives understanding
(discernment and comprehension) to the simple.

PSALM 119:130 AMPC

Dear good, gracious heavenly Father, sometimes it is so dark here. Not just the darkness of night or storm or interiors; the darkness of sin and unknowing presses close. I am reaching up for Your light in the only way I can. Thank You, Lord, for Your Word. It comforts and illuminates in a way that nothing else does. It makes You present and real to me. I praise You for giving me something that is so *alive* with Your Spirit to be my anchor and lantern in the darkness. Amen.

Day 141

CONFIDENCE

*Therefore I say unto you, What things soever
ye desire, when ye pray, believe that ye
receive them, and ye shall have them.*

Mark 11:24 kjv

Thank You, Father, that I can come to You in confidence. I am so unworthy to be able to be given access to You through prayer, yet You delight in the communication we have. When I bring requests to You, I want those requests to be things that are not selfish or outside of Your will. Grant that my desires are Your desires, Father. I know that You will always give me whatever I truly need.

Day 142

SEEDLINGS

And he took the children in his arms,
placed his hands on them and blessed them.

MARK 10:16 NIV

Dear Father, I know my children give You as much joy as they give me, and I just want to thank You for them today. Thank You for their quick minds, their healthy bodies, their loving hearts, their hilarious antics. Most of the time I'm so busy feeding, teaching, disciplining, and organizing them that I don't take even a moment to praise You for what awesome creations they are. Each unique and precious, and each with a soul that will live forever. Give me grace as I continue to point their hearts to You. Amen.

Day 143

TOMORROW

Take therefore no thought for the morrow: for the morrow shall take thought for the things of itself.

MATTHEW 6:34 KJV

The truth is that I have no control over tomorrow, Lord. Free me from worries about the future, whether tomorrow or next week or next year. May I rely on You today so that I can focus on the here and now, this moment, and trust You to take care of whatever comes next. I do trust You, Father. Help my actions be evidence to that fact. I yearn for the freedom that comes from being worry-free!

Day 144

HEART'S DESIRE

*Delight thyself also in the LORD: and he
shall give thee the desires of thine heart.*

PSALM 37:4 KJV

Thank You, God, that You created the deepest, truest
desires that live within me. You have made me uniquely
different from everyone else, and You've given me
a desire to live inside Your will. Thank You for the
passions and gifts You have given me. Please show
me ways that I can use those gifts to be a blessing to
You. I'm glad that as I delight in You, I can trust You
always to meet the needs of my yearning heart.

Day 145

THE PAST IS GONE

As far as the east is from the west, so far has He removed our transgressions from us.

PSALM 103:12 NKJV

Father, I'm glad You have redeemed my past. I've said and done things of which I'm not proud. I'm grateful that You've blotted out my sins and given me a fresh start. Like one using a marker board, You wiped away the shame and guilt and handed the marker back to me. I don't have to live in the past; I can face the future with confidence and grace. In Christ's name, amen.

Day 146

TRANSPLANTED

Instead, they were longing for a better country—a heavenly one. Therefore God is not ashamed to be called their God, for he has prepared a city for them.

HEBREWS 11:16 NIV

Dear God, You know I am about to move *again*. Even though this is a move I've been waiting, hoping, and longing for, it will still be stressful. Please be with me in this transition. Amid all the plans and packing, I pray that You would help keep my eyes focused on You. No matter where I put down roots for the next year, or ten or twenty, my true home is in heaven and my true roots in Christ alone. Amen.

Day 147

OPEN UP WIDE!

I am the LORD thy God, which brought thee out of the land of Egypt: open thy mouth wide, and I will fill it.

PSALM 81:10 KJV

Lord, like a baby bird, I will open wide my soul's mouth, knowing that You will always feed me all I need. Open up my heart today, God, and fill it to the brim with just what I need: encouragement, joy, a spirit of servanthood, a passion for the lost, patience, kindness, and a love for others. I'm ready, Father—fill me up!

Day 148

A PERFECT PLACE

Now I saw a new heaven and a new earth, for the first heaven and the first earth had passed away.

REVELATION 21:1 NKJV

Creator God, I wish there weren't diseases in our world. Those tiny microbes that infiltrate the immune system are responsible for so much pain and grief. Although sickness was not present in the Garden of Eden—that perfect place You intended for us—it is a part of this life now, a consequence of the curse under which our world suffers. But someday You'll create a new earth, and I know bacteria won't stand a chance there. I look forward to that, Father God, for then the world will once again be "very good." Amen.

Day 149

SATISFIED

*And the LORD shall guide thee continually, and
satisfy thy soul in drought, and make fat thy bones:
and thou shalt be like a watered garden, and
like a spring of water, whose waters fail not.*

ISAIAH 58:11 KJV

Even in the midst of life's droughts—when everything
seems dry and dead and dusty—thank You, Father, that
You continue to water my heart and satisfy my soul.
When I see others are in the midst of drought, give
me the right words and actions to share Your living
water that will keep them from ever being thirsty again.

Day 150

WEEDS

*For wisdom is better than rubies, and all the things
one may desire cannot be compared with her.*

PROVERBS 8:11 NKJV

Dear Lord, You are the master Gardener. I love to plant
flowers, vegetables, bushes, and bulbs, but nothing in
my garden can compare with the glory that was Eden.
My garden is nothing like that perfection. If I ignore
it for two weeks, weeds spring up; in two months,
it would be a jungle. My life is just like my garden,
Lord. Sometimes new things seem insignificant at first:
a new TV program, a new book, a new acquaintance,
a new train of thought. But they can grow rampantly.
Give me wisdom to recognize weeds when they are
small and pluck them out. Amen.

Day 151

HUNGRY SOULS

For he satisfieth the longing soul,
and filleth the hungry soul with goodness.

Psalm 107:9 kjv

God, my soul gets so hungry for You sometimes. I know that it's not You who has moved away, but the problem is with me. Thank You that You are immovable, unshakable, and always there. Because of this, I know just where to run to find You to satisfy my longing soul. Give me a firm footing in Your presence so I am not tempted to wander away again. Thank You for being patient with me.

Day 152

INTERNAL CLOCKS

*To declare Your lovingkindness in the morning,
and Your faithfulness every night.*

PSALM 92:2 NKJV

Heavenly Father, it seems like every person has an internal rhythm seemingly permanently set to a certain time in the day. There are early birds and night owls and middle-of-the-day people. Not many of us are successful in changing our internal clock, Lord. Maybe You wanted to create humans with varying peak hours of energy. It would be a pretty boring world if we all fizzled out at the same time each day. Thank You for the variety You have provided in all of us. Amen.

Day 153

ROOTSTOCK

*Know therefore that the L*ORD *your God is God;
he is the faithful God, keeping his covenant
of love to a thousand generations of those who
love him and keep his commandments.*

DEUTERONOMY 7:9 NIV

Dear Father, You are a God who is faithful from generation to generation. Thank You for the men and women in my family tree who loved You and passed a godly heritage down to my parents and to me. I praise You that You are the same yesterday, today, and tomorrow: You are the same God Abraham worshipped four thousand years ago, that Paul worshipped two thousand years ago, that my great-grandfather worshipped one hundred years ago. And I praise You that my children and their children's children can follow the same unchanging God. Amen.

Day 154

RICH IN GRACE

In whom we have redemption through his blood, the forgiveness of sins, according to the riches of his grace.

EPHESIANS 1:7 KJV

The world tells me I should be rich in material wealth, Father, but true riches are found in Your limitless grace. Thank You for the richness of Your grace, Lord. Thank You that Your grace is large enough to cover all my past sin, my current sin, and my future sin. That's the kind of rich inheritance I truly desire!

Day 155

WATERED

He dawns on them like the morning light
when the sun rises on a cloudless morning,
when the tender grass springs out of the
earth through clear shining after rain.

2 SAMUEL 23:4 AMPC

Dear Father, I thank You for things that reach upward, that remind me to lift my arms in praise. Mountains, trees, clouds: they all reach higher than my little arms, but only I can praise You. When I praise You, Lord, I feel so different: washed clean with joy and somehow taller. I feel like a plant after a spring rain. I praise You for the beauty of the earth, the skies, and the heavens, and for Your great love, which surrounds and sustains it all. Amen.

Day 156

PROMISES

This is my blood of the new testament,
which is shed for many for the remission of sins.

MATTHEW 26:28 KJV

Jesus' blood is the new testament—the new promise You have made to me, Lord. I am not bound by the rules and regulations of the Old Testament law, but instead I have been given amazing freedom! The blood of Jesus is so powerful that I cannot comprehend it, but please help me to always rely on His saving blood that heals all my sins.

Day 157

FITNESS

"Physical training is good, but training for godliness is much better, promising benefits in this life and in the life to come."

1 Timothy 4:8 nlt

It's an exercise-crazy world we live in, Lord. Gym memberships are prized, morning jogs are eulogized, and workout clothing has become a fashion statement. There are some who make this area of self-care too important; they spend an inordinate amount of time on it. Yet others don't keep it high enough on their priority list. Help me, God, to keep the proper perspective of fitness, because, after all, I have a responsibility for the upkeep on this body. It's on loan from You. Amen.

Day 158

WILDER

*By faith Abraham obeyed when he was called to go out
to the place which he would receive as an inheritance.
And he went out, not knowing where he was going.*

HEBREWS 11:8 NKJV

Dear God, today I ask You for strength. I need Your
strength to break old habits of sin that are holding me
back from the freedom You promise me in Christ. The
devil wants me tame: a creature fully at his bidding.
Only You, God, give me the capacity to grow and
change and stretch. I ask for Your courage today as I
abandon old patterns and step past the borders of what
is easy and familiar into the wild, beautiful country
beyond. Help me to trust that even if it looks like I
am the only one following this path, You are guiding
me every step of the way. Amen.

Day 159

FAITHFUL

If we confess our sins, he is faithful and just to forgive us our sins, and to cleanse us from all unrighteousness.

1 JOHN 1:9 KJV

God, I confess to You that I have sinned. I have gone astray, away from Your love. Again and again I fall short. It shames me to admit it, but You ask for my confession. Forgive me. Wash me. Bring me home. Thank You that even now, I can rely on Your faithful love. Thank You for the promise that You are faithful to forgive me—not just yesterday and today but tomorrow as well.

Day 160

STAKED

*The eternal God is your refuge and dwelling place,
and underneath are the everlasting arms.*

DEUTERONOMY 33:27 AMPC

Lord, the wind is howling like a beast around the house right now. Everything that is not nailed down tight rattles and moans. Our house can stand this much wind, Lord, but how much *more* before it whirls away? Sometimes, Lord, when the wind howls so and reminds me of my frailty, I wonder how long *I* can hold on. How many more tragedies, trials, and temptations? But then You are there, beloved Savior, reminding me of the everlasting arms that are always around me, comforting, sustaining, and protecting. Thank You, Jesus. I stake my life on You. Amen.

Day 161

POWER

The Son of man hath power on earth to forgive sins.

MARK 2:10 KJV

Jesus, no one else has the power to forgive sins like You do. You took the shame of my sins on Your shoulders as You hung on the cross. I cannot understand the immense pain and suffering You endured as You were beaten and ridiculed. You paid for me. You took care of my insurmountable debt. Thank You for Your sacrifice, and thank You for Your power that sets me free from my sins.

Day 162

SLICE OF LIFE

Make the most of every opportunity in these evil days.
EPHESIANS 5:16 NLT

Dear Lord, the transition of minutes to hours is so incremental that it is tedious to observe. It's much easier to focus on a large chunk of time than a myriad of tiny ones. Yet hours are made up of minutes, just like the body is comprised of cells. Each is vital to the whole. Lord, help me remember that each minute of the day is a small section, a slice of my life. Help me make the best use of every minute. Amen.

Day 163

GOD'S NAME

Help us, O God of our salvation, for the glory of thy name: and deliver us, and purge away our sins, for thy name's sake.

PSALM 79:9 KJV

I know that my sins make me dirty, God. More than that, my sins separate me from You. But because You are who You are, You make me clean, Lord. You cover me in the blood of the Lamb, and You deliver me from all my sin so that I may dwell in Your presence. It's nothing that I've done on my own. May I always bring Your name glory!

Day 164

NOURISHED

There are different kinds of gifts, but the same Spirit distributes them. There are different kinds of service, but the same Lord. There are different kinds of working, but in all of them and in everyone it is the same God at work.

1 CORINTHIANS 12:4–6 NIV

Dear Father, I thank You for Your church. I have worshipped You and listened to teaching from Your Word in so many different buildings, but the same Spirit has filled them. I know I could walk into any Bible-believing church in Seoul, Zanzibar, Toledo, or Des Moines and feel immediately at home. That is because You are there too. I thank You for the church I am a part of right now. I pray that You would bless all the people who serve there with extra measures of Your joy, strength, and love this week. Amen.

Day 165

A JOB FOR ME

*"But seek first the kingdom of God
and His righteousness, and all these
things shall be added to you."*

MATTHEW 6:33 NKJV

Dear heavenly Father, I need a job. You know the challenges I'm facing in my present situation. You understand the reasons why I need to make this change. There are so many people looking for work; employers have a large pool from which to draw. Still, You've promised to supply my basic needs if I would keep Your kingdom top priority in my life. So, I ask that You would direct my search and help me approach this transition with integrity and consideration for my present employer. I ask this in Your name, amen.

Day 166

PURGED

Iniquities prevail against me: as for our
transgressions, thou shalt purge them away.

Psalm 65:3 kjv

I mess up a lot, Father. In fact, sin seems stronger than me sometimes, dear Lord. It takes such a steady foothold in my life that I feel powerless to change. Purge away this tendency from my heart, I pray. I will focus on You and Your Word, Savior God, and I know that You will lead me away from the temptation of sin.

Day 167

BACKSLIDING

O Lord, though our iniquities testify against us, do thou it for thy name's sake: for our backslidings are many; we have sinned against thee. . . . Thou, O Lord, art in the midst of us, and we are called by thy name; leave us not.

JEREMIAH 14:7, 9 KJV

No matter how far along I go in my spiritual walk with You, Lord, sooner or later I always start to slide backward. There are some temptations and situations that will always make me struggle, and I admit that sometimes I succumb to those temptations and sin. And yet You are here with me. Don't leave me now.

Day 168

GARDENING

*For the Son of man is come to seek
and to save that which was lost.*

LUKE 19:10 KJV

Dear Lord, other people's lives can be so messy. Like a teenager's room, it's tempting to close the door and ignore what is inside. But You are a God who is not afraid of messes. You are not afraid to reach into the tangles and the mire. You see into the future of a lost person's heart: You see a garden where I only see a dangerous wilderness where *I* might get hurt—or simply dirty. Lord, I want to be like You; I want to love the lost like You do. Help me to look past the mess to the eternal soul inside. Amen.

Day 169

GETTING STARTED

The way of the sluggard is blocked with thorns.

PROVERBS 15:19 NIV

Dear Lord, the first step toward any goal is the hardest, and I just don't feel motivated to take it. But there are things I need to do, and so far I haven't found a fairy to do them for me. Procrastination is a terrible hindrance. I know. I'm a closet procrastinator. I don't like to admit to it, but You see it anyway. Thank You for giving me more chances than I deserve. Remind me that I just need to start. Inspiration often springs from soil watered with obedience. Let me learn this lesson well. Amen.

Day 170

REBELLION

To the Lord our God belong mercies and forgivenesses, though we have rebelled against him.

DANIEL 9:9 KJV

Sometimes I act like a two-year-old or a teenager—I want to do what I want to do when I want to do it. I disregard what I know is right and good and travel down a dangerous path. Even when I'm in the middle of the situation, I know I'm doing wrong. I rebel against Your love, Lord. Thank You that despite my sheer stupidity, You always forgive me, even though I don't deserve it. Help me never take advantage of Your forgiveness.

Day 111

HARVEST

For this is good and acceptable in the sight of God our Savior, who desires all men to be saved and to come to the knowledge of the truth.

1 TIMOTHY 2:3–4 NKJV

Dear Lord, I thank You that the other night a little girl I love prayed in the dark with her older sister to ask You into her heart. I thank You that other children are asking their friends from school to youth group and that they are getting *saved*. I thank You for the teenagers of a dear friend who love You more than anything in their lives. I thank You for a girl who prays for her grandmother's salvation every day. Lord, the fields are white unto harvest, and You are lifting up faithful laborers even among the little ones. Amen.

Day 172

EMPLOYER WOES

*Whatever you do, work at it with all your heart,
as working for the Lord, not for human masters.*

COLOSSIANS 3:23 NIV

God, I have the most demanding boss ever. I need to demonstrate the love of Christ, but it can be challenging when my superior is, at times, so hard to please. Give me courage, Lord, to rise above my emotions. Help me pray for my boss as the Bible tells me to and serve as though it is an assignment from You. For You, Lord, are my true superior. Bless my boss today, God, and show Your love to him through me. Amen.

Day 173

MERCIFUL

I will be merciful to their unrighteousness, and their sins and their iniquities will I remember no more.

HEBREWS 8:12 KJV

Thank You that You are a merciful God. You don't even remember all the many times I let You down! You truly forgive and forget. Teach me how to show this kind of mercy to people in my life who have wronged me—that I may shine Your light to others in a real and genuine way, with unconditional love.

Day 174

DIFFICULT PEOPLE

Bear with each other and forgive one another if any of you has a grievance against someone.

Colossians 3:13 niv

Dear Lord, I ask You to help me be patient and kind today. The Bible speaks about long-suffering. That's what I need as I deal with difficult people and irritating situations. Whether it's squabbling children or rude drivers or harried clerks, I know there will be those today who will irk me. In those moments when I want to scream, help me remember to forbear and forgive. It's just so easy to react, but help me instead to deliberately choose my response. I'm depending on Your power, Father. Amen.

DELIGHTED IN MERCY

Who is a God like unto thee, that pardoneth iniquity, and passeth by the transgression of the remnant of his heritage? he retaineth not his anger for ever, because he delighteth in mercy.

MICAH 7:18 KJV

Father, sometimes when I seek Your forgiveness for a sin that I commit over and over again, I assume that while You are still forgiving me, You might be doing so begrudgingly. But the truth is that You delight in mercy! So You delight in forgiving me? What an amazing thought! What would I do without Your mercy?

Day 176

BIRDSONG

*"The LORD your God in your midst, the Mighty
One, will save; He will rejoice over you with
gladness, He will quiet you with His love,
He will rejoice over you with singing."*

ZEPHANIAH 3:17 NKJV

Lord, I praise You for the little birds in my garden:
the chickadees, the robins, the juncos, the purple
finches. I praise You for the evening song of the hermit
thrush. They are like sequins on a glorious world!
You've thought of everything, Lord, and You rejoice
in it. Help me remember that as much as I rejoice in
songbirds, You rejoice in me even more. Because I am
of more value than many sparrows. But thank You for
the sparrows too. Amen.

Day 177

BLOTTED OUT

I, even I, am he that blotteth out thy transgressions
for mine own sake, and will not remember thy sins.

Isaiah 43:25 kjv

God, I'm so thankful that You don't hold grudges. I give You thanks and praise, dear Lord, for You have not only wiped away all my sins but You also don't even remember them! You wipe my slate clean; You give me a new start; You hit the Reset button. You have made me truly free from the past.

Day 178

INSURMOUNTABLE DISTANCE

As far as the east is from the west, so far hath he removed our transgressions from us.

PSALM 103:12 KJV

Whenever I feel that I'm a hopeless case, that I'll never be able to rise above the sin that I fall into, remind me, Father, that from Your perspective, my soul and my sin might as well be in different dimensions, separated by an insurmountable distance. Take away my shame and guilt that I feel about my past sins, and help me rest in the fact that I am completely forgiven.

Day 179

GOOGOLPLEX

He telleth the number of the stars; he calleth them all by their names. Great is our Lord, and of great power: his understanding is infinite.

<small>Psalm 147:4–5 kjv</small>

Lord, You are infinite and beyond comprehension. I *know* this with my head, but infinity is such a non-human sort of concept! I try to think about You in this way, but my mind keeps trying to reduce You to something smaller, something I can wrap my understanding around. I praise You that You are wholly infinite and infinitely holy. Who is like You? I don't understand, but I rest, a speck in Your loving hand. Amen.

Day 180

BEHIND GOD'S BACK

*Thou hast in love to my soul delivered it
from the pit of corruption: for thou hast
cast all my sins behind thy back.*

Isaiah 38:17 KJV

I have to imagine that if You put something behind
Your back, Creator God, it doesn't really even exist
anymore. You don't want to look at it, think about it,
or even be bothered by it. Always remind me that this
is what You have done with my sins! I am free!

Day 181

GRACE IN THE NOT-KNOWING

So when. . .this mortal has put on immortality,
then shall be brought to pass the saying that is
written: "Death is swallowed up in victory."

1 CORINTHIANS 15:54 NKJV

Lord, tonight I've cried and cried, and You've listened and loved me and given me words of truth and comfort. But I'm still confused. Someone I love is with You tonight. This morning she was with her husband and children. I wonder why You didn't heal her, because I know You could have and I thought You were going to! Why, Lord? I don't know how to rejoice that she is walking on streets of gold and at the same time weep that her children will grow up without her. But I rest in Your sovereignty, Lord. Please help me live with grace in the not-knowing. Amen.

Day 182

UNLIMITED RESOURCES

*"For every animal of the forest is mine,
and the cattle on a thousand hills."*

PSALM 50:10 NIV

Father, the Bible says You own "the cattle on a thousand hills." You have unlimited resources. So I'm asking You to supply a special need I have today. Although I try to be a good steward of the money You give me, some unexpected event has caught me without the necessary funds. I know You can remedy this situation if You deem that good for me. Because You're my Father, I'm asking for Your financial advice. I need Your wisdom in this area of my life. Amen.

Day 183

THE DEPTHS OF THE SEA

*He will have compassion upon us; he will
subdue our iniquities; and thou wilt cast
all their sins into the depths of the sea.*

Micah 7:19 kjv

Thank You for Your loving compassion, heavenly
Father, that throws my sin to the bottom of the
darkest, deepest ocean—never to be thought of
again. Take all the selfish urges of my heart and subdue them so that I may be free to serve You as I
long to.

Day 184

GOD IS A SHIELD

*He shields all who take refuge in him. . . . He trains
my hands for battle; my arms can bend a bow of
bronze. You make your saving help my shield.*

PSALM 18:30, 34–35 NIV

Protector God, today I'm remembering someone in
the armed forces. Though I know war wasn't in Your
original plan for this world, it has become a necessary
tool for overcoming evil. The Bible recounts stories of
You leading Your people, the Israelites, into battle to
defend what was right. So there is honor in defending
freedom and justice. I ask You to protect this one from
danger; dispatch Your peace, and put a hedge before,
behind, and around him. Watch over all those who are
putting their lives in harm's way for my sake. In Christ's
name, amen.

Day 185

THE RESCUE

"He rescues and he saves; he performs signs and wonders in the heavens and on the earth."

DANIEL 6:27 NIV

Dear Father, tonight I watched a movie in which a sweet but foolish girl was kidnapped and sold into slavery in a foreign country. No one would help her, except her father, who crashed through every barrier and mowed down every bad guy who stood in his way. Though stabbed, beaten, and broken, he found her and rescued her and brought her home. I just started weeping, Father, when I realized that *this* is exactly what You have done for me. I was lost and alone and sold into slavery in this sin-stricken world. You *came*. You rescued me. Thank You again and again. Amen.

Day 186

NEW CLOTHES

Take away the filthy garments from him.
And unto him he said, Behold, I have caused
thine iniquity to pass from thee, and I will
clothe thee with change of raiment.

ZECHARIAH 3:4 KJV

Lord, You offer me a brand-new wardrobe to replace my filthy clothes that are stained with sin. Forgive me when I wrongfully believe that my dirty rags are adequate and I try to hold on to them. Help me put on the new clothes You hold out to me. Dress me in Your love and forgiveness.

Day 187

COMMUNICATION

I will set nothing wicked before my eyes.

PSALM 101:3 NKJV

Dear God, the internet is a marvelous tool! Thank You for giving humankind the ability to invent it. But the internet also has a great potential for evil. I ask You to protect my family from online predators, from sexual content, from sites that would have a negative influence on our relationship with You. Help me be prudent in my use of the web. Like any other means of communication, it can be used wrongly. But, with Your help, it can be an instrument for good in our home. Amen.

Day 188

SHOWERED

*Then will I sprinkle clean water upon you,
and ye shall be clean: from all your filthiness,
and from all your idols, will I cleanse you.*

EZEKIEL 36:25 KJV

Each time I take a shower, God, remind me that You have showered my soul with Your love. As I lather up with soap that will cleanse the dirt of the day, remind me of the cleansing power of Your grace and mercy. You have washed away everything in me that was false, and now I am truly clean.

Day 189

CROCUSES

For the LORD thy God bringeth thee into a good land, a land of brooks of water, of fountains and depths that spring out of valleys and hills.

DEUTERONOMY 8:7 KJV

Dear Lord, I just want to praise You today for the surprising ways You love us. Thank You for the way rain droplets spangle a branch like diamonds. Thank You for a stranger's unexpected smile in a busy store. Thank You for the pictures You paint every evening at sunset. Thank You for clear, rushing streams and cold drinks of water. Thank You for the bright heads of crocuses that spring out of the dregs of winter. Thank You for how You delight in surprising me with the beauty of Your Word and Your world. Amen.

Day 190

WHENEVER I PRAY

And when ye stand praying, forgive, if ye have ought against any: that your Father also which is in heaven may forgive you your trespasses.

MARK 11:25 KJV

Whenever I come to You, Lord, asking You to grant me some request, remind me first to let go of any unforgiveness I'm holding in my heart. I don't want to be a grudge holder, and I know that withholding forgiveness hurts me more than it hurts the other person. Show me ways to show true grace—Your grace—to others who have hurt me.

Day 191

THE TERRIBLE MERCY

"Though he slay me, yet will I hope in him."

JOB 13:15 NIV

Dear Lord, I just finished thanking You for the little moments of beauty You gift me with every day. Then, suddenly, as the sunset faded, the horror of this world seemed to hit me along with the darkness. There are crocuses and raindrops and smiles, but there are also broken bones and broken marriages, breast lumps and biopsies, wars and widows. It's so hard to know what to do with all this beauty so inextricably mixed up with all this viciousness. I am crying out to You. Help me trust Your love even as I try to understand it, Lord. Amen.

Day 192

A SHINING LIGHT

"Let your light so shine before men, that they may see your good works and glorify your Father in heaven."

MATTHEW 5:16 NKJV

Dear God, I want to be a better witness for You. I have friends and family members who don't know You, and every day I interact with people who aren't believers. Lord, I don't want to be corny or pushy, but I do want to let my light shine before others. I ask You to open up the doors for me today. Let me sense Your prompting. And let the silent witness of my life also speak to others about Your great plan of salvation. In Jesus' name, amen.

Day 193

ANGER DEFERRED

The discretion of a man deferreth his anger;
and it is his glory to pass over a transgression.

PROVERBS 19:11 KJV

The word *glory* refers to the essence of something, the quality that makes it give forth light. Dear God, remind me that I am most truly myself, my best and shiniest self, when I don't act on my anger against others. Give me the wisdom to know how to react to people and situations in the same way You would react. Let love, respect, and kindness be at the root of everything I do.

STILL LEARNING

Above all, love each other deeply, because love covers over a multitude of sins.

1 PETER 4:8 NIV

Lord, I'm really ticked at my husband right now. I just don't get it. How can he be unaware of how his insensitive words hurt me? What I really want to do is quote all those Bible verses to him—the ones that say "love your wives" and "be not bitter" (Colossians 3:19 KJV). But I know You're the only One who can really speak to his heart. Please open his understanding to the way words affect me as a woman. Teach him how to be gentle. And help me remember I'm also a student in relationships. May we both let *You* control the classroom! Amen.

Day 195

HOLES

He also brought me up out of a horrible pit. . . . He has put a new song in my mouth—praise to our God; many will see it and fear, and will trust in the LORD.

PSALM 40:2–3 NKJV

Dear Lord, You know where I was when You found me: at the bottom of a hole so deep even the end of my rope was out of reach. All I wanted to do was pull the dirt down on my own head and die. But You didn't let me. And You didn't just reach down to me; You jumped *in*. Verses, people, hymns, moments of unexpected beauty—they all showed me that You were right there with me, loving me, lifting me. Thank You for changing the ending of my story, Lord, and giving me a tale to tell to the lost. Thank You for the transformative power of Your love. Amen.

Day 196

PERSECUTION

Do good to them that hate you, and pray for them which despitefully use you, and persecute you.

MATTHEW 5:44 KJV

Father, bless all those who have hurt me, all those who have hurt those I love, all those who have hurt the innocents of our world. I ask that You show me how to reach out my hands in kind and practical ways to these individuals who have brought hurt into our world. Help me to see past their actions to their own hurt. Use me to show them Your mercy and love.

Day 197

BLESSINGS INSTEAD OF CURSES

Bless them that curse you, and pray for them which despitefully use you.

LUKE 6:28 KJV

My Lord, I feel misused. I feel cursed. I feel slighted and abused. I'm angry and hurt. I come to You with these feelings, and I give them to You. Take away the hurt and my desire for revenge. Give me Your heart when it comes to others. I pray that You would bless the people who have made me feel this way. Your will be done, Father.

WARMING MY HANDS BY HOLY FIRE

For our God is a consuming fire.

HEBREWS 12:29 NKJV

Dear Lord, it's so cold this morning. Frost covers the ground, and the air is as still as ice. My fingers are cold too, but I thank You for a warm cup of tea and a house with a furnace. You always provide for me and protect me, Lord. I never need to worry. Thank You that Your love doesn't wax and wane like the warmth of the sun through the seasons. You are a constant and faithful source of light and warmth for my soul. Don't let me grow cold, Lord, but keep my hands pressed up against Your blaze. Amen.

I BLEW IT

If we confess our sins, He is faithful and just to forgive us our sins and to cleanse us from all unrighteousness.

1 John 1:9 nkjv

Lord, I blew it today. I was unkind to my husband and harsh with my kids. I wish I could take back my attitude and words. Sometimes it's difficult for me to understand why You still love me. I am so thankful You would trust me with a family, even though I've done a pretty terrible job of nurturing today. Please forgive me. Your Word promises me cleansing if I confess. Help me remember this the next time I feel frustrated and impatient. Help me exercise my will and choose to respond appropriately to the family You've given me. In Christ's name, amen.

Day 200

INHERITANCE OF BLESSING

*Not rendering evil for evil, or railing for railing:
but contrariwise blessing; knowing that ye are
thereunto called, that ye should inherit a blessing.*

1 PETER 3:9 KJV

It's my first reaction to strike back when I'm hurt, to complain against people who complain about me. You know those tendencies within me, Father. Turn them inside out, I pray, and may my first reaction instead be always to pray and bless. When I feel that this is too much to ask of me, remind me that You will give back to me countless blessings in return.

LITTLE CREAKS DOWN THE STAIRS

But it is good for me to draw near to God:
I have put my trust in the Lord GOD,
that I may declare all thy works.

PSALM 73:28 KJV

Dear Father, I can't count how many times I've just sat down at my desk with my Bible and a cup of coffee when I hear the telltale, hesitant creaks on the stairs indicating the approach of a small person who isn't sure of his reception. I confess, Lord, that my heart sinks. But I want more than anything to be like You, and I know that there is never a time when I reach out to You and Your heart doesn't *leap*. I want my children—and the other people around me—to understand the depth of Your love. Help me show them, in part, through the depth of *my* love for them. Amen.

Day 202

PUTTING UP WITH IT!

Being reviled, we bless;
being persecuted, we suffer it.

1 Corinthians 4:12 kjv

God, give me patience to put up with all the grief that comes my way! You know the things that push my buttons, that get under my skin. Give me the peace to endure them. I know You will use the situation according to Your will, but it's not so fun to suffer through it! Give me the comfort and encouragement I need to endure.

HOW DO I LOVE THEE?

"For God so loved the world that He gave His only begotten Son, that whoever believes in Him should not perish but have everlasting life."

JOHN 3:16 NKJV

Dear God, *love* is such a little word, just four letters—a greeting card, fairy-tale, romance novel word. I say *I love hamburgers* with the same verb I would use to say *I love Jesus*. Most of the time, I don't think about the power of that word: how it can move mountains, calm storms, heal lepers, redeem a sinner. That word saved me from hell. I remember when I first fell in love, how I longed to hear that word back from my beloved. And that earthly love is just a dim shadow of what You feel for me. I love You, Lord. Let me never stop counting the ways. Amen.

Day 204

KEEP ME

Keep me as the apple of the eye,
hide me under the shadow of thy wings.

PSALM 17:8 KJV

Dear Father, in the scurry of life, I often forget to be thankful for important things. So many times You've shielded my family from physical harm, and I didn't know it until later. And I'm sure I don't even know about all those moments when You've guarded us from spiritual danger. Although we are the apple of Your eye, I realize we're not immune to trauma and disaster; You won't remove the effects of the curse until the right time comes. But for now, I'm grateful that You care about us and that the only way something can touch us is after it's passed Your gentle inspection. Amen.

Day 205

FEEDING MY ENEMIES

*Therefore if thine enemy hunger, feed him;
if he thirst, give him drink.*

ROMANS 12:20 KJV

It's not enough to *forgive* my enemies, Lord; now You ask me to actively do them good—to do whatever I can to meet their needs. I'm hurting so much right now that I can't do this on my own, Father. Show me how You want me to do that, and then give me the strength to do it. May I look for opportunities to help those who have hurt me.

Day 206

IN THE NEIGHBORHOOD

*Who is a God like You, who pardons iniquity
and passes over the rebellious act of the remnant
of His possession? He does not retain His anger
forever, because He delights in unchanging love.*

MICAH 7:18 NASB

Dear Father, I am surrounded on all sides by people who are dangerously close to spending eternity away from Your presence. They are one misstep (a fall off a ladder, a stumble into traffic) from an eternity they cannot even imagine. I would run into the road to stop a man from being hit by a car; I would scream to wake a woman asleep in a blazing house. But when it's a question of eternity, I say nothing. Open my eyes, Lord, to the moments when the enemy's lying tongue is quiet, and give me Your Words to say. They are just one *prayer* away from an eternity they cannot imagine. Amen.

Day 207

WAITING FOR GOD

Say not thou, I will recompense evil; but wait on the LORD, and he shall save thee.

PROVERBS 20:22 KJV

When a situation arises where wrong has been done, I'm quick to feel that the situation is urgent: I have to do something about it *right now*. Teach me, Lord, to wait for You instead. Give me Your wisdom in these situations, and when the time is right, show me what to say and what to do that will bring glory to You.

Day 208

SIBLING REVELRY

Whoever claims to love God yet hates a brother or sister is a liar. For whoever does not love their brother and sister, whom they have seen, cannot love God, whom they have not seen.

1 John 4:20 niv

Heavenly Father, thank You for my siblings. When the chips are really down, I can depend on them. They know my background, my temperament, and my journey. We share the same blood and the same basic life philosophy. When we were kids, we squabbled a lot; but now, I just love getting a call from one of them. They understand me like no one else. And I pray we'll always be there for one another. Bless my brothers and sisters today. In Jesus' name, amen.

Day 209

HE IS WILLING

Jesus reached out his hand and touched the man. "I am willing," he said. "Be clean!" Immediately he was cleansed of his leprosy.

MATTHEW 8:3 NIV

Dear God, You love us so much that You were willing to leave Your kingly throne and come down into the muck and the sin. For a holy God, sin is *worse* than leprosy. I'm not a leper, *exactly*. My face isn't marred by open sores; I'm not missing pieces of my lips and nose. But sometimes my face *is* mottled by anger, and I'm missing large chunks of the love, joy, peace, patience, kindness, goodness, faithfulness, gentleness, and self-control that are my birthright in Christ. Again and again, You are willing to reach out and touch me and cleanse me with Your amazing love. Thank You, Jesus.

THE OTHER CHEEK

*Whosoever shall smite thee on thy right
cheek, turn to him the other also.*

MATTHEW 5:39 KJV

Really, God? If someone hurts me, do I really have to ask him to hurt me again somewhere else? That seems like You're asking too much! It goes against everything society teaches me about standing up for myself, about being assertive, about not being a doormat. Teach me what Jesus meant when He said this. Give me a heart that wants to follow His example. . . even when I don't want to.

Day 211

FOLLOWING GOOD

See that none render evil for evil unto any
man; but ever follow that which is good,
both among yourselves, and to all men.

1 THESSALONIANS 5:15 KJV

Even when I see evil all around me, Lord, help me
to always follow that which is good rather than evil.
Forgive me when I am lured by the fake shininess and
beauty that evil displays. Keep me from falling for the
tricks of the devil, and keep my feet securely on Your
path, the good and right path.

Day 212

THE PROMISE KEEPER

*For no matter how many promises God
has made, they are "Yes" in Christ.*

2 Corinthians 1:20 niv

Dear Father, how many times have I promised (even just to myself) to call someone and didn't? How many times have I promised to play dolls with my little girl or read a story to my son and didn't? How many times have I promised to get a certain job done and didn't? Forgive me for breaking those promises. You are a God who keeps His promises, who is faithful from generation to generation. Teach me what it means to be truly faithful. Amen.

Day 213

ROLE REVERSAL

"Even to your old age, I am He, and even to gray hairs I will carry you! I have made, and I will bear; even I will carry, and will deliver you."

ISAIAH 46:4 NKJV

Dear Lord, when I was growing up, my parents seemed ageless. But I realize now that my time with them is getting shorter every day. They're getting older, Lord, and, more and more, I find myself looking out for them. This role reversal is really difficult for me. I'm accustomed to them looking out for me, and part of me wishes I could stay in their care for a while longer. Please give me strength to deal with this new phase of our relationship, and help me honor them as long as they live and beyond. Amen.

Day 214

LOVE

[Love] beareth all things, believeth all things,
hopeth all things, endureth all things.

1 Corinthians 13:7 kjv

Give me a loving heart, God. Help me to endure hurts, always hoping and believing in the best in others. Remind me that love is an everyday action, not just when I feel like it. Help me show love in words as well. Give me Your eyes to see the true worth of the people around me, and help me to always display Your love to them. Thank You for being the perfect example of love.

THE ETERNAL SECURITY SYSTEM

*For He will give His angels [especial] charge over
you to accompany and defend and preserve you
in all your ways [of obedience and service].*

PSALM 91:11 AMPC

Dear Lord, Your Word says that we are protected, all
unawares, by Your mighty angels. They accompany us
and defend us and preserve us when we are walking in
Your way. This is not just another security system with
a little picture of an angel to stick in our front lawn
to deter criminals; they don't just sound an alarm in
heaven when our walls have been breached. They keep
evil *away*. I know there have been times in my life when
You protected me, and I was very aware of it. Thank
You, Lord. Thank You also for the invisible guardians
that surround me and defend me from the evil I never
even see. Amen.

Day 216

SPIRITUAL GUARDRAILS

*Stay alert! Watch out for your great enemy,
the devil. He prowls around like a roaring
lion, looking for someone to devour.*

1 PETER 5:8 NLT

Dear God, help me erect proper boundaries in my life. I don't want to fall prey to a sin simply because I wasn't being careful. Just like guardrails on a dangerous mountain highway, boundaries in my life keep me closer to center and farther away from the cliffs. I know Satan is plotting my destruction, but Your power is greater. Let me cooperate with Your grace through a careful lifestyle and a discerning spirit. In Christ's name, amen.

Day 217

QUARRELS

Forbearing one another, and forgiving one another, if any man have a quarrel against any: even as Christ forgave you, so also do ye.

<small>COLOSSIANS 3:13 KJV</small>

Quarrels come so easily some days, Lord, especially with the people I live and work with the most closely. Remind me that Christ has forgiven me for far greater offenses, and help me bite my tongue before I start an argument. When I do stumble and take part in a fight, help me be humble and ask for forgiveness from the other person. Grant me freedom in my relationships so I am not distracted by bitterness.

Day 218

RULE OF LOVE

"To him who sits on the throne and to the Lamb be praise and honor and glory and power, for ever and ever!"

REVELATION 5:13 NIV

Dear Lord, You are Lord of the universe, yet You left Your throne and came down to earth to be near us. You are the giver and sustainer of life, yet You sacrificed Your Son to save us. You are the King of kings, yet You put aside Your crown to become one of us. There is no precedent for this kind of love. The president of the United States wouldn't sacrifice his child for peace in the Middle East or send his child to live with beggars in Venezuela so they could learn about democracy. That would never happen. What You did for us makes no earthly sense. But You did it, and I am forever grateful. Amen.

Day 219

TENDERHEARTED

And be ye kind one to another, tenderhearted,
forgiving one another, even as God for
Christ's sake hath forgiven you.

EPHESIANS 4:32 KJV

The world may look at a tender heart as a weakness, but You know better, God. Your heart is tender toward me, and You are quick to extend grace and mercy. Give me a tender heart, I pray. Guard my heart so that it won't become calloused to the hurts and evils of the world. Fill me with Your kindness, gentleness, compassion, and sincerity so that I can forgive others just as I have been forgiven.

Day 220

MOTHER

"As one whom his mother comforts,
so I will comfort you."

ISAIAH 66:13 NASB

Dear Lord, I thank You today for my mother. No one else except You has loved me like she has. From before I was born, through sickness and rebellion, and even when I was thousands of miles away, she has loved me. You blessed me so much when You gave me to this particular woman. I praise You for her gentleness, generosity, and quiet strength. I pray that You would bless her today, Lord, with the awareness of how her love and Yours have made a difference in eternity. Amen.

Day 221

OVERCOMING

Be not overcome of evil,
but overcome evil with good.

ROMANS 12:21 KJV

When darkness seems to be attacking me from all sides, Lord, give me Your strength so that I can rise above the world's evil. Make Your Spirit strong in me so that I can feel Your presence near. Give me the words to say and the things to do to bring Your goodness to every situation. Use me in whatever way You can for Your will to be done. I know I'm on the winning side!

IN ANY AND EVERY SITUATION

From the fruit of their mouth a person's stomach is filled; with the harvest of their lips they are satisfied.

PROVERBS 18:20 NIV

Dear Lord, right now my belly is full and my body is well rested, and I confess that I confuse that physical contentment with spiritual health. And at other times I have believed the lie that aches, pains, and sickness mean You have withdrawn Your hand of blessing from me. Neither is necessarily true, as You make abundantly clear in Your Word. Paul had a thorn in his flesh, while the healthy and wealthy You struck down. Conversely, demons caused sickness, and You blessed Solomon with great wealth. Help me live in the light of eternity, unswayed by bank balances, buffets, or blood tests. Amen.

Day 223

PASSION AND PURPOSE

In Him also we have obtained an inheritance, being predestined according to the purpose of Him who works all things according to the counsel of His will.

EPHESIANS 1:11 NKJV

Father, I'm in a rut. I like some familiarity, but this monotony is wearing away at my sense of purpose. I know there are parts of our lives that are not particularly glamorous, fulfilling, or significant (at least, on the surface). Yet living without passion or purpose isn't what You had in mind for us. Show me, Lord, how to find meaning in my everyday life. Open up to my eyes the subtle nuances of joy folded into life's mundane hours. I put my longings into Your hands. Amen.

GOD'S CHILDREN

Be ye therefore followers of God, as dear children.
EPHESIANS 5:1 KJV

Brothers and sisters often bicker and squabble. My siblings and I are no exception. But remind me, dear God, that Your children should be following You, not fighting with each other. Grant us an abundance of grace when we are dealing with each other, and help us keep our eyes solely on You as we work through difficulties. If we are following Your will, we will be blessed beyond imagination.

PASCAL'S PUZZLE

*Once you were alienated from God. . . . But now
he has reconciled you by Christ's physical body
through death to present you holy in his sight,
without blemish and free from accusation.*

COLOSSIANS 1:21–22 NIV

Dear Lord, Blaise Pascal once wrote that there is a God-shaped hole inside every person. I know I felt it and tried to fill that hole with so many things besides You: work, school, achievement, friends, parties, travel. But nothing was a perfect fit, and the hole remained. But when You found me, even though in pride and fear I tried to say no, the piece that was missing clicked into place. I thank You, Lord, for that hole, for showing me that I was created for something different than a "normal" life. Stop me, Lord, if I lose my first love and start filling that hole with something besides You. Amen.

Day 226

MERCIFUL

Be ye therefore merciful,
as your Father also is merciful.

LUKE 6:36 KJV

Father, I am so thankful for Your mercy, and I am thankful for Your gift of grace—but You know that it is sometimes difficult for me to show mercy to others. It's especially hard for me to be merciful when I see someone making the same mistake over again or committing the same sin again and again. But right now I pray that You make me like You. Help me show Your mercy to everyone—with no exceptions.

AT DAWN IN EDEN

*And they heard the sound of the LORD God
walking in the garden in the cool of the day.*

GENESIS 3:8 NKJV

Dear Father, I have always longed to be in the Garden
of Eden in those first days when You walked with
Adam and Eve in the cool of the day. You enjoyed Your
creation; You thought it was beautiful. You enjoyed
Your creatures, especially Your people, and You wanted
to spend time with them. I am so sorry for what we
lost, and I know You are too. We lost the completeness
we had in Eden; we lost that perfect garden and that
perfect fellowship with You. But the gift is not like
the trespass. Thank You that what You gave us in Jesus
Christ is even more beautiful than what we lost. Amen.

Day 228

CHEERFULNESS

"Be of good cheer, daughter."
MATTHEW 9:22 NKJV

Jesus, I can't imagine You as a sour, solemn man. I believe You enjoyed life immensely, and I know You brought joy to those around You. Why else would "sinners and tax collectors" want to eat with You (as Your enemies pointed out)? Your mission on this planet was sacred and grave, but I believe Your demeanor in everyday life was buoyant and pleasant. Others loved being in Your presence. Help me pattern my daily attitude after Your example and take heed of Your command to "be of good cheer." Let me reflect You by the way I approach living. Amen.

Day 229

SEMPER PARATUS

*"But rise and stand on your feet; for I
have appeared to you for this purpose,
to make you a minister and a witness."*

ACTS 26:16 NKJV

God, today I have felt like a concrete footing when
the forms get removed. Am I dry and sturdy? Will I
stand on my own? Will I support a structure above
me? I confess that I've been depending on the faith
and scripture knowledge of people around me instead
of developing my own. When I stand before You, You
aren't going to ask whether I was the cousin of a Bible
scholar or married to a person of great faith. You will
see *me*. I long to hear You say, "Well done." Increase
my faith and devotion to You. Amen.

Day 230

SHIELDED

Above all, taking the shield of faith,
wherewith ye shall be able to quench
all the fiery darts of the wicked.

EPHESIANS 6:16 KJV

Lord, You tell me that my faith is a shield that will protect me from evil. Right now I ask You to reinforce that shield. Give me a greater, stronger faith so that I will be ready when I go through difficult times, when Satan is shooting his fiery darts directly at me. I will not live in fear about this possibility, but I will stand on Your promises.

ESSENTIAL JESUS

*They replied, "Believe in the Lord Jesus, and you
will be saved—you and your household."*

Acts 16:31 niv

Lord, I see in myself the tendency to become a
Pharisee: to add rules to the essential simplicity of
the Gospel. Sometimes I wonder if maybe I need to
dress differently, read only a certain translation of
the Bible, talk with a more specialized "Christian"
vocabulary. But then You remind me of Acts 16:31.
"Believe in the Lord Jesus." "Be saved." That's it. It's
not esoteric knowledge; it's not an unattainable level
of enlightenment; it's not dressing a certain way; it's
not a thousand-mile pilgrimage: it's just You, Jesus.
Help me stay true to this message by staying close to
You. Amen.

Day 232

GOD'S GENTLENESS

Thou hast also given me the shield of thy salvation:
and thy gentleness hath made me great.

2 SAMUEL 22:36 KJV

Father God, when I think about Your gift of salvation to me, I think about the mighty work that Your grace through the death of Jesus Christ does in my life. But there's another side to it. God, thank You for Your gentleness that makes me strong enough to rise above every trial that comes my way. It's because I am saved that I can be free to stand and not be afraid.

Day 233

QUIET AND GENTLE

The unfading beauty of a gentle and quiet spirit. . .is of great worth in God's sight.

1 Peter 3:4 niv

God, I read in Your Word that You value spirits that are gentle and quiet. At times, this is oh so hard for me, Lord! I'm not a total pushover, and I do have my own opinions about things. Sometimes it is so hard to keep quiet or speak softly. Yet, Lord, You know that I want to be that way. The universe has enough bossy women. Teach me, Lord, how to be quiet and gentle. Amen.

Day 234

GOD'S ARMOR

But let us, who are of the day, be sober,
putting on the breastplate of faith and love;
and for an helmet, the hope of salvation.

1 THESSALONIANS 5:8 KJV

Father, remind me not to venture out into life's temptations and trials without first putting on Your armor, especially the breastplate of faith and love and the helmet of Your salvation. Teach me to grab hold of these gifts and harness the power that You offer through them. Give me the opportunity to use these pieces of armor to bless others, protecting them against the power of evil.

Day 235

THE ALREADY-DONE LIST

The LORD appeared to him from afar, saying, "I have loved you with an everlasting love; therefore I have drawn you with lovingkindness."

JEREMIAH 31:3 NASB

Dear God, I love plans and schedules. They help me stay focused and productive and turn the 1,440 minutes in each day into goals set and attained. But I know I have missed opportunities to deepen relationships because I was too busy checking off boxes on my to-do list or too rigid to change plans at the last minute. And I know that often I base my idea of how much *I* am worth on how much I have been able to accomplish. Help me remember that I can never *do* enough to earn Your love. I am already loved, completely and eternally. The only thing that really needed doing, You did on the cross. Thank You, Lord.

A QUIET QUEST

"In quietness and confidence shall be your strength."
ISAIAH 30:15 NKJV

Dear Lord, we all find great blessings when in the company of others, enjoying those times when we are with people. But I need Your help to embrace solitude too. Let me see the value in spending some time alone, giving my mind time to decompress, refreshing my spirit in the quiet. Not only do I need to spend quiet time with You in personal worship, but I also need to incorporate into my daily routine those pockets of time when the music is off and the computer is down. Help me make times of quiet my quest. Amen.

Day 231

LIT

*Let your loins be girded about,
and your lights burning.*

LUKE 12:35 KJV

When everywhere I look I see only darkness, please, Lord, turn on the lights in my heart. Show me ways to share that illumination with everyone around me. When Your light burns, darkness flees. Use me. Light me, I pray.

Day 238

WIDE AWAKE

Therefore let us not sleep, as do others;
but let us watch and be sober.

1 THESSALONIANS 5:6 KJV

You know how tired I am, God. You know how weary I am of facing troubles and challenges. Help me not surrender to my exhaustion. Send godly friends into my life who can encourage me to continue on the path that You have laid for Your children. Keep me wide awake and alert, focused always on You.

CRY IN THE NIGHT

*"Then you call on the name of your god,
and I will call on the name of the LORD.
The god who answers by fire—he is God."*

1 KINGS 18:24 NIV

Dear Lord, there is never a time I cry out to You and You are not instantly listening. Unlike the false god of the prophets of Baal, You are never busy, traveling, sleeping, or too deep in thought to hear me. The only thing that stops my prayers from reaching You is my own unconfessed sin. Help me examine my heart when I fear that You are silent, and forgive my sins. I long to stand before You, complete and unashamed. Just as I run to my baby when he cries, I know I am never alone. Amen.

Day 240

DELIVERED

Because he hath set his love upon me, therefore
will I deliver him: I will set him on high,
because he hath known my name.

PSALM 91:14 KJV

When troubles threaten to drown me, loving Lord, reach down and save me. Deliver me from the floods. Rescue me from the fire. Remove me from the storm. Protect me from the violence. Pick me up and set me on a high place where I will be safe in Your presence. I know my Deliverer is coming.

Day 241

BLESSED ARE THE FLEXIBLE

This is the day the LORD has made;
we will rejoice and be glad in it.

PSALM 118:24 NKJV

Flexibility is a struggle for me, God. I don't like interruptions in my routine. It's challenging for me to accept a rerouting of my day. Still, sometimes You have to reorganize for me because I haven't recognized Your promptings. Or maybe there's someone You need me to meet or a disaster You want me to avoid. Help me accept the detours in my plan today, aware of Your sovereignty over all. Amen.

Day 242

PRESERVED

The LORD preserveth all them that love him.

PSALM 145:20 KJV

Preserve me, God; keep me safe—that's what I'm asking of You. Guard my physical body, my head, and my heart. Grant me travel mercies as I move from place to place. Take away my anxiety, my worries, and my woes. I love You—and I need Your help now. I can't do it alone.

THE LIAR

If we confess our sins, he is faithful and just to forgive us our sins, and to cleanse us from all unrighteousness.

1 JOHN 1:9 KJV

Dear God, someone I care about told me a lie today—in church, no less. It was a small lie about an insignificant thing, but it felt like a brick had been thrown at me. I carried that brick like an ugly goblin baby—a changeling—all through the service; and the music, the sermon, the fellowship of other believers were soured for me because of my burden. Then I realized, Lord, because You so lovingly showed me, that the burden had become mine because I chose to carry it. Thank You for showing me how to lay that ugly thing at the foot of the cross and pick up joy instead. Amen.

TRUE HOMELAND PERSPECTIVE

They agreed that they were foreigners and nomads here on earth. Obviously people who say such things are looking forward to a country they can call their own.

HEBREWS 11:13–14 NLT

God, I want to live with an eternal perspective. Heaven is more than a feel-good fable for the graveside. It's an actual place, as real as this earth and far more lasting. When I live like this earth is the ultimate goal, I tend toward selfish indulgence. When I remember that heaven is my real destination, I put value on the lasting things, the things of true importance. Remind me to keep an eye toward Your heavenly kingdom. Amen.

THE ONE NEEDFUL THING

I will be fully satisfied as with the richest of foods;
with singing lips my mouth will praise you.

PSALM 63:5 NIV

Dear Father, You are the giver of good gifts, but I confess that I'm often on the lookout for more. I go to the store, Lord, and all the things I see look so nice and necessary. They are just sitting there on the shelves, but in my mind, they are jumping up and down, dancing, and waving to get my attention: *Hey, pick me! No, me! I'll make you happy! I'll make you thinner! Take me with you!* Thank You for the things I have, but help me control my desire for more. No *thing* I have will defile me, but neither will it make me complete. Only You can make me complete, Jesus. Amen.

Day 246

ALIVE AND BLESSED

The Lord will preserve him, and keep him alive;
and he shall be blessed upon the earth: and thou
wilt not deliver him unto the will of his enemies.

PSALM 41:2 KJV

Sickness. . .violence. . .exhaustion. . .stress: our world is full of dangers. Some of the dangers I face are truly life-threatening, Lord. But I don't want to live a life of fear. You call me to be bold and fearless. Thank You that You've promised to not only save my life but also to bless me.

THE PERFECTIONIST TRAP

As for God, His way is perfect.
2 Samuel 22:31 ampc

Dear Lord, I am so glad that You are such a high, mighty, and separate God. I praise You that You are not like the gods of the Vikings or the Greeks, quarrelsome tricksters and schemers. We can only make gods in our own image. We could never imagine You, Lord. I would never bow to Artemis or Baal or Thor, but I realized just now in my perfectionism I am setting up another god to worship—myself. Always doing, striving, perfecting, tweaking my little universe. Please help me be content with imperfection. Only You are perfect, and I am now complete in You. Amen.

Day 248

NEVER FORSAKEN

For the LORD loveth judgment, and forsaketh
not his saints; they are preserved for ever.

PSALM 37:28 KJV

Father God, I've experienced abandonment in my life. The experience left me feeling empty, alone, helpless. Thank You, Father, that You will never forsake me; You will never abandon me. I am grateful for the security this promise affords me. You will keep me safe forever in Your loving arms that are big enough and strong enough to hold me and all my issues.

Day 249

JUST DO IT

But be doers of the word, and not hearers only, deceiving yourselves.

JAMES 1:22 NKJV

Dear Lord, I want to have an obedient heart. Sometimes, when You speak to me, I feel hesitation or want to postpone what You're telling me to do. Yet that means either I don't trust You or I want my own way, neither of which is good. A child ought to obey her parents because she acknowledges their right to direct her and because she trusts the love behind the words. Help me, Lord, to embrace that kind of attitude when You speak to me. In Christ's name, amen.

Day 250

SAVED FROM ALL EVIL

The LORD shall preserve thee from all evil: he shall preserve thy soul.

PSALM 121:7 KJV

Evil comes in so many shapes and forms. Sometimes it comes into my life disguised, and by the time I recognize its presence, my soul is already in danger. When this happens, Father, be my rescuer (even when I don't ask for rescuing!). Thank You, Lord, that You are always watching over me—and You will protect me from evil of every kind.

Day 251

MY HIDING PLACE

*Thou art my hiding place; thou shalt
preserve me from trouble; thou shalt compass
me about with songs of deliverance.*

PSALM 32:7 KJV

Heavenly Father, when the world seems like a dangerous place, when anxieties rush at me everywhere I turn, be my hiding place. Be by my side, and let me run into Your arms. Wrap me up in Your embrace, and sing to me Your sweet song of deliverance. May I never think I'm so self-sufficient that I reject Your comfort and protection, Daddy.

Day 252

FRESH INK

I lean on, rely on, and trust in Your word.
PSALM 119:42 AMPC

Dear Lord, I pray for insight today as I read Your Word. Open it to me, Lord, and reveal Your heart to me. I confess that it has not been my meat and drink as it should. I want to know You better today than I did yesterday and better tomorrow than I do today. Thank You for the Holy Spirit, who guides me as I read, and I pray for a fresh filling of that Spirit. You make all things new, Lord, and I thank You for the verses I will read today and how they will speak to me, as if You wrote them for me this morning, as if the ink is still wet. Amen.

Day 253

THE SIMPLE LIFE

Aspire to lead a quiet life, to mind your own business, and to work with your own hands.

1 Thessalonians 4:11 nkjv

Dear God, *simplicity* is a buzzword today. It seems everyone wants "simple" in some fashion. Perhaps it's because life has become too complicated for many of us; we yearn for a more laid-back lifestyle. Lord, I need to simplify my goals in my relationships and my work. Doing so will help me to have a more laser-like focus. And in my spiritual life, a little simplifying might be good too. Instead of daily reading numerous chapters of Your Word, help me to concentrate on one or two verses, thus deepening my understanding of You. Lord, help me keep simple goals and a simple faith as I simply live for You. Amen.

Day 254

A TOWER ON A ROCK

The God of my rock; in him will I trust: he is my shield, and the horn of my salvation, my high tower, and my refuge, my saviour; thou savest me from violence.

2 SAMUEL 22:3 KJV

You, Lord, are my place of absolute safety: a high tower built on a rock that will never move. When trials and temptations surround me, teach me to lift my gaze higher. Help me look above all my troubles and see Your tall tower—and then run there as fast as I can!

Day 255

MIRROR, MIRROR

*I will praise You, for I am fearfully
and wonderfully made.*

PSALM 139:14 NKJV

Father, when I look at certain people I know, all I see is how much I lack in comparison. They seem naturally kinder, more at ease, more fashionable, more attractive, and certainly thinner. I know, Lord, I often spend more time thinking about how other people see me than about how You see me. You made me, sovereign Lord, in this particular way for Your purposes. Help me trust You, and trust that this lump of clay that You are molding is precious in Your sight and in Your hands. Amen.

THE PATH TO JOY

*Keep your lives free from the love of money
and be content with what you have.*

HEBREWS 13:5 NIV

Lord, I live in a culture that demands more. Wherever I look, I see glossy advertisings of things I "need." It's difficult to be content when you're bombarded with messages to the contrary. But I know that accumulating more stuff isn't the path to joy. And You don't bless me so I can indulge myself, but so I can share with others. Let my life be marked by restraint and a deep contentment that's rooted in You, the center of my fulfillment. In Jesus' name, amen.

Day 257

MY REFUGE

The LORD also will be a refuge for the oppressed, a refuge in times of trouble.

PSALM 9:9 KJV

In times of trouble, Lord, when I feel that the pressure is overwhelming, thank You that You are my Refuge—a place of peace, love, and acceptance. Teach me to seek Your protection at the onset of troubles rather than trying to handle them on my own. I don't get extra points for trying to stick it out by myself.

Day 258

WHERE'S YOUR MISSING PIECE?

In Him you have been made complete.

COLOSSIANS 2:10 NASB

Dear Lord, the people who still need You don't usually advertise it out loud. They don't usually go around with "Unsaved" or "Missing Jesus" emblazoned on their T-shirts. Sometimes they look just fine, like they aren't missing anything at all. Lord, this is when I feel most uncertain how to tell them about You. I need Your eyes, Lord, to see exactly where and how deep are their "God-shaped holes." Unbelievers are not complete, despite how they may appear. I trust You to lead me for You love them so much. Amen.

TIME MANAGEMENT

*Teach us to number our days, that we
may gain a heart of wisdom.*

PSALM 90:12 NIV

Dear God, sometimes I think I need more than twenty-four hours in my day! It seems I never have enough time. I think with longing about simpler seasons in my life, when I could actually complete my to-do lists. There was such satisfaction in having a few stress-free moments. Now, my schedule is filled, and I'm so harried. Holy Spirit, please guide in this area of my life. How I use my time is part of stewardship, so I'm asking for Your wisdom. Show me how to manage the hours I have so I can honor You in everything I do. In Christ's name, amen.

Day 260

SINGING

But I will sing of thy power; yea, I will sing aloud of thy mercy in the morning: for thou hast been my defence and refuge in the day of my trouble.

PSALM 59:16 KJV

God, You know all the troubles that surround me—but today I'm going to start my day singing. Give me a song of power and mercy that will stay with me all day long, especially when the stresses of the day come. No matter what life throws at me, I want to live with Your joyful melody in my heart until Jesus returns to take me home!

Day 261

HOPE

*Thou art my hiding place and
my shield: I hope in thy word.*

PSALM 119:114 KJV

God, I know that one of the surest ways to find Your hope is to open up scripture and meditate on Your Word. There I learn that You thought of me at the beginning of creation, that You formed me in my mother's womb, that You love me and cherish me, that You provided a way for me to have an intimate relationship with You through the death, burial, and resurrection of Jesus Christ, and that You have amazing plans for me here and into eternity. Your words fill me with amazing hope, Father.

Day 262

MY PRAYER WARRIORS

Always labouring fervently for you in prayers, that ye may stand perfect and complete in all the will of God.

Colossians 4:12 kjv

I thank You, Lord, today for all the people who have prayed for me. I am humbled by how I have been surrounded, from the day I was born, by people who have lifted me up to the throne of grace, faithfully and passionately. I may not ever know who they are, but I ask You to bless them today. Strengthen their faith in the invisible power of their work. I ask that You would bring me to their minds today, Lord, for I covet their intercession. Thank You for these faithful warriors. I need them so desperately. Amen.

Day 263

SAFE IN THE MIDST OF THE WORLD

*I pray not that thou shouldest take
them out of the world, but that thou
shouldest keep them from the evil.*

JOHN 17:15 KJV

Jesus, You didn't ask that I be physically removed
from the earth so that I'd be immune to the world's
temptations and tests. Instead, You asked that God
protect me no matter what I face. Thank You, Jesus,
that You prayed for *me*.

Day 264

THE UNVEILING

But we all, with unveiled face, beholding as in a mirror the glory of the Lord, are being transformed into the same image from glory to glory.

2 Corinthians 3:18 nasb

Lord, I'm wondering what it really means to be complete in Jesus Christ. What does *complete* really mean for me? Whole. Absolute. Total. Finished. Accomplished. Concluded. Fulfilled. Done. These are all synonyms, and I am struck by their common sense of finality. There is nothing left to be done. My transformation from stone to flesh was finished at the cross. The work is done; we are just awaiting the final unveiling. Praise Jesus. Amen.

Day 265

YES AND NO

But let your communication be, Yea, yea; Nay, nay:
for whatsoever is more than these cometh of evil.

MATTHEW 5:37 KJV

God, teach me Your ways so that no evil will take root
in my life. Remind me to make my word count so that
my "yes" means yes and my "no" means no. Make me
a person of integrity whom others can trust. When
people ask me why I do what I do, let me always point
them to You.

Day 266

THE WELL OF WORDS

"Whoever drinks the water I give them will never thirst. Indeed, the water I give them will become in them a spring of water welling up to eternal life."

John 4:14 NIV

Lord, You've given me a love of words, and by Your grace, You've allowed me to use it. Sometimes, though, I worry that I'll run out of things to say. What if the well runs dry? But then I remember how You created everything out of nothing. You spoke, and it came to be. You are the author of life, the Word made flesh. Thank You for breathing that same spark of creativity into us along with the breath of life. I know that if I keep my eyes fixed on You, I'll never run out of words. There is no end to the ways I can praise You! Amen.

Day 267

BACK TO CENTER

*Mark out a straight path for your feet
so that those who are weak and lame
will not fall but become strong.*

Hebrews 12:13 nlt

Heavenly Father, I need balance in my life. It's one of the hardest things for humans to achieve. We're so prone to lopsidedness, to extremes. Maintaining center is challenging. That's why I need You to straighten me out and help me stay in the narrow way. In those areas of my life where I'm listing to the side, bring me back to center, Lord. In Jesus' name, amen.

Day 268

CLOTHED IN TRUTH

Stand therefore, having your loins girt about with truth, and having on the breastplate of righteousness.

EPHESIANS 6:14 KJV

Father, this world has exchanged truth for lies. What You see as black and white, society sees as gray. Right and wrong have been twisted in such a way that many people are confused and don't even know *what* to think. Today I ask that You clothe me in truth so that I can live as You want me to. Give me the boldness to stand up for what is right and in love guide others to You, the ultimate source of Truth.

Day 269

TIME MACHINE

*There is a time for everything, and a season
for every activity under the heavens.*

ECCLESIASTES 3:1 NIV

Dear Lord, I have so much work to do each day and so
little time. I always feel like I'm running behind. It's a
treadmill, Lord, set on a speed that's just a little too fast
for me to keep up. I'm always just on the verge of flying
off the back into a heap on the floor. But I know this
is not what You want. Jesus was a man who was never
in a hurry. He had just enough time to do the Father's
will. He had time to pray on a mountainside, time to
chat beside a well, time to sit by a lake and cook a fish
with friends. Give me wisdom as I seek to set aside my
endless to-do list for Your holy will. Amen.

Day 270

HOPE TO THE END

*Wherefore gird up the loins of your mind, be sober,
and hope to the end for the grace that is to be
brought unto you at the revelation of Jesus Christ.*

1 PETER 1:13 KJV

I have put my hope in Your grace, Lord, which You showed to me through the life of Your Son, Jesus Christ. The account of His death, burial, and resurrection is one that saves me for all of eternity. Meanwhile, I want to emulate His example of grace-filled living now, in my everyday life. Help me always to keep His example as my focus.

Day 271

HOSPITALITY

Use hospitality one to another without grudging.

1 Peter 4:9 kjv

Dear Lord, I need to improve my skills in hospitality. Because You have blessed me, I need to share with others. In fact, hospitality is one of those virtues the apostle Paul commanded of the church. Sharing my home with others is my Christian duty and also a great way to reach out to unbelievers I have befriended. Please let me not dread hosting others but rather find ways to make it doable and enjoyable for all. In Jesus' name, amen.

FIRM

But the Lord is faithful, who shall stablish you, and keep you from evil.

2 THESSALONIANS 3:3 KJV

God, I know You are faithful. Be my Rock and my firm foothold, and please be the foundation of my life. Make me firm and solid, so that I can always resist evil. When my own faith is firmly rooted, then please allow me to help others find their strength in Your faithfulness. Your strength will sustain all Your children!

Day 273

THE BEACON

*No one has seen God at any time. If we
love one another, God abides in us, and
His love has been perfected in us.*

1 JOHN 4:12 NKJV

My family isn't perfect, Lord. You know how often
selfishness, angry words, hurt feelings, and laziness
mar our relationships with each other. You know how
we are when the door is shut and no one is watching.
But we love You, and You are teaching us to love.
Increase our love; let it shine out for everyone around
to see. Make us a light on a hill, Lord, so that those in
darkness would see our Jesus. Amen.

Day 274

NO SLIPPING

He will not suffer thy foot to be moved:
he that keepeth thee will not slumber.

PSALM 121:3 KJV

I'm coming to a situation in my life where the way ahead looks slippery and dangerous, Lord. Please hold my hand, and when necessary, pick me up and carry me. I know that You won't leave me or even take a break to get a little rest. Thank You that I can rest in You even during difficult stretches of the path.

Day 275

THE REAL ME

I have chosen the way of truth.

PSALM 119:30 NKJV

Heavenly Father, so many people in my world wear masks. We earth dwellers are afraid to be real with others; we fear losing the respect and esteem of our peers. And, oddly enough, we're often afraid to be real with even You—and You know everything about us anyway. I want to be genuine in my approach and interaction with others, including You. Give me the courage to reject the lure of artificial "perfectness" and instead live out my life and relationships in a real way. Amen.

Day 276

COBWEBS OF THE SOUL

*"You will keep him in perfect peace,
whose mind is stayed on You."*

Isaiah 26:3 nkjv

Dear Father, You know how good I feel when my house is in order, when the floors are swept, the bathrooms are clean, the beds are made, and the toys are picked up. It imparts an order and peace to my soul. And You know how I feel when chaos reigns: scattered, bewildered, short-tempered. Help me remember that it is no different with my spiritual house. Help me keep the cobwebs and confusion in check with daily prayer, study, and meditation on Your Word. And thank You that I *can*. Amen.

STRAIGHT WAYS

Lead me, O Lord, in thy righteousness because of mine enemies; make thy way straight before my face.

PSALM 5:8 KJV

God, You know how hard it is for me sometimes to know which way I should go. Today I ask that You be my map and my guide. Please show me clearly the way You want me to follow. Remind me that You've already "been there and done that." While I may question why we're going a certain way, You know what is best, and You have great plans for me.

ACCOUNTABILITY

*The L̶ord̶ will be at your side and will
keep your foot from being snared.*

PROVERBS 3:26 NIV

How many times, Lord, have I heard about Christian
leaders who fell into great sin. I may have read their
books, seen them on TV, and then suddenly their
life and ministry crumbled to bits when sin that was
hidden came to light. Those leaders probably never
imagined where their sin would take them, and I
thank You for reminding me that I too am capable of
any sin. Please protect me, Lord. Surround me with
people who will ask tough questions about my life
and hold me accountable. I want to be useful to You,
Lord, not a broken object of scorn and pity. Amen.

Day 279

PLAIN PATHS

*Teach me thy way, O LORD, and lead me in
a plain path, because of mine enemies.*

PSALM 27:11 KJV

I need Your help, Lord. I can't see which path I should take. It's dark, I'm confused, and the enemy of my soul has hidden Your way from me. Please, Lord, lead me—and remove the evil that is in the way!

Day 280

WALKING IN TRUTH

Teach me thy way, O LORD; I will walk in thy truth: unite my heart to fear thy name.

PSALM 86:11 KJV

I am guilty of having a divided heart, God. I want to do Your will, but I also want my will to be done. Forgive me for my selfishness. When my heart feels torn with conflicting desires, Father God, please unite me so that I have a single focus in life: Your way, Your truth, Your will, Your path.

Day 281

A DREAM DEFERRED CAN BLOOM

He hath made every thing beautiful in his time.

ECCLESIASTES 3:11 KJV

When I feel small and insignificant, Lord, You so graciously remind me of this verse. When I remember the goals and dreams I had when I was younger that I have not achieved because I chose to follow You instead, You remind me where true worth lies. Thank You for the contentment that only comes from following You. But I thank You too for how You are fulfilling some of my old dreams in unexpected ways. I love You, and I trust You completely. If my heart is set on You, then what You give me *will* be the desire of my heart. Amen.

Day 282

FRIENDS FOR EVERY NEED

A time to weep, and a time to laugh;
a time to mourn, and a time to dance.

ECCLESIASTES 3:4 NKJV

Dear heavenly Father, I am grateful for my friends. They are such a vital part of my life. When my family can't be there, my friends come through for me. When I need someone to gripe to, they will listen. When I need a kick to get me going again, they don't hesitate. My journey through life would be so lonely and unhappy without these amazing women who walk it with me. Thank You for blessing me through them. Help me return the favor. Amen.

Day 283

MORNING LOVE

Cause me to hear thy lovingkindness in the morning;
for in thee do I trust: cause me to know the way
wherein I should walk; for I lift up my soul unto thee.

PSALM 143:8 KJV

It is my desire, Father God, to meet You in prayer every morning. As I start out each day, give me ears, loving Lord, to hear Your voice—and then may I listen for that still, small voice all through my day. Follow me into the evenings and whisper loving thoughts to me at night as I rest my head, ready to meet You again in the morning.

Day 284

DISGUISES OFF!

For now we see through a glass, darkly; but then face to face: now I know in part; but then shall I know even as also I am known.

1 CORINTHIANS 13:12 KJV

Lord, You have let me be part of the most amazing thing in the world—Your church. Where believers gather, You are present, and Your glory is made visible. I confess that often I don't even try to look with Your eyes. I see an old building full of strange people doing odd things. I need to see with Your eyes: that our hundred-year-old church is really a shining fortress, that our creaky voices are a descant to the most glorious choral music in the universe, that the retired accountant in the pew behind me is really a warrior in brilliant armor. And I am something more than I appear. Help me retrain my eyes, Lord, to see as You do. Amen.

Day 285

GOD'S EYE

I will instruct thee and teach thee in the way which thou shalt go: I will guide thee with mine eye.

PSALM 32:8 KJV

I have a dog that follows the direction of my gaze and knows what I want her to do. All I need to do is look at her bed for her to go there and lie down. If I look in another direction, toward a treat I've hidden for her, she leaps up and runs to the morsel of food. Lord, help me to be as responsive to Your gaze. Keep me so tuned in to You that You can use Your eyes to show me where You want me to go.

A CAGED BIRD SINGING

Rejoice to the extent that you partake of Christ's
sufferings, that when His glory is revealed,
you may also be glad with exceeding joy.

1 PETER 4:13 NKJV

Dear God, I want to thank You for Paul and Silas. Seized and hauled through the marketplace, stripped and beaten with rods, thrown into prison—they prayed and sang hymns from their jail cell. Your Word says the other prisoners were *listening* to them: listening and learning what it means to serve a risen Savior. Nothing like that has ever happened to me, Lord, and I am very grateful. I have never felt the terror of a mob; I have never felt the touch of an angry hand; I have never been in prison. My trials are ordinary. But I pray that, even still, I would be faithful to praise You in them—because people are listening. Amen.

Day 287

MOVING AND MAKING FRIENDS

A man who has friends must himself be friendly.

PROVERBS 18:24 NKJV

God, I don't like change or new places. I'd rather just stay in my comfort zone. But that's not happening. Here I am in a strange new environment. I miss my old friends so much. I feel like crying just thinking about them. But that won't do any good, will it? I need some heavenly moxie. It's time to square my shoulders, walk in, smile, introduce myself, and meet some new people. I guess I can think of them as prefriends. Help me not to chicken out! Thank You. Amen.

Day 288

FOR MY OWN GOOD

*Thus saith the LORD, thy Redeemer, the
Holy One of Israel; I am the LORD thy God
which teacheth thee to profit, which leadeth
thee by the way that thou shouldest go.*

ISAIAH 48:17 KJV

Sometimes I forget, Lord, that Your guidance is always
for my good. I admit that sometimes it feels a little bit
like taking my medicine. But You want what's truly best
for me. Your paths always lead me to joy and blessing
and health. Teach me to trust You more fully today
and every day.

Day 289

OPEN EARS

*And thine ears shall hear a word behind thee,
saying, This is the way, walk ye in it, when ye turn
to the right hand, and when ye turn to the left.*

ISAIAH 30:21 KJV

Give me sharp ears, heavenly Father, so that I can hear
Your voice. Tune my ears to be receptive to only You,
and give me discernment so I can disregard the false
voices that may try to imitate You.

THE PROOF IS IN THE PUDDING

*"Then you will know the truth,
and the truth will set you free."*

JOHN 8:32 NIV

Dear Father, we are a gullible people. From the very beginning, we were tricked and led astray. Satan whispered in Eve's ear, she listened, and everyone ever since has been falling for his lies. *Just this once. It doesn't really matter. I deserve this. No one will find out.* We believe his lies about everything from eating too much chocolate, to "borrowing" a pencil from work, to committing adultery or murder. I am no different. I need You every moment, Lord, to help me sort through the chatter in my head so I can be certain what to listen to and what to stand against. Only the truth. Only what glorifies You. Amen.

Day 291

RECONCILIATION

Be kind to each other, tenderhearted, forgiving one another, just as God through Christ has forgiven you.

EPHESIANS 4:32 NLT

Dear Lord, I feel as if I'm on the set of *I Love Lucy* today, starring in an episode in which Ethel and Lucy have had a quarrel. I just can't believe that my friend and I had this disagreement. It feels so odd to have a chill between us instead of the warm camaraderie we've always shared. I confess I'm still hurt over what she said. Maybe she feels the same about the words that came out of my mouth. So please help us both to take the steps toward reconciliation. What do You want me to do right now to start repairing this friendship? Amen.

Day 292

NO MORE CROOKED WAYS

I will bring the blind by a way that they knew not; I will lead them in paths that they have not known: I will make darkness light before them, and crooked things straight. These things will I do unto them, and not forsake them.

ISAIAH 42:16 KJV

Sometimes my life's path seems to take one unexpected turn after another. I feel as though I'm stumbling through a dark maze. One day though, Lord, when I look back at my life from heaven's perspective, I will see that You made my life's crooked paths run absolutely straight, right to You!

LITTLE MARY, QUITE EXTRAORDINARY

"For He who is mighty has done great things for me, and holy is His name."

LUKE 1:49 NKJV

God, thank You so much for Mary, this nobody of a girl from nowhere who became the mother of God. I thank You for her amazing example of humility and exuberant praise. She never drew attention to herself; instead, everything she said glorified You. She lived a poor, quiet life but found favor in Your eyes and became a witness to the Incarnation, the defining event of history. Only You, Lord, delight in turning our expectations on their head this way! Help me be more like Mary, Lord, and say continually, "Let it be to me according to your word" (Luke 1:38). Amen.

Day 294

THE PATH OF LIFE

Thou wilt shew me the path of life: in thy presence is fulness of joy; at thy right hand there are pleasures for evermore.

PSALM 16:11 KJV

Why do I think I'm a trailblazer, Lord? Sometimes my way seems better to me, so I take a little side trip off Your path, only to find disappointment, destruction, and heartbreak. I know that only Your path, God, leads me to life. . .to joy. . .to pleasures that will last forever. I will put blinders on my eyes, Father—looking straight ahead to You.

Day 295

FAITHFUL FRIENDSHIP

Faithful are the wounds of a friend.

PROVERBS 27:6 NKJV

Father, I need to confront my friend. She seems to be making some bad decisions. I'm so afraid for her. Please keep me from joining in the discussions of others who are talking about her. Yet my just being silent isn't what she needs. I know some things about her life that have brought her to today; I know her secret pain and longings. Let me not betray her but rather come alongside to share the burden she's carrying and perhaps lovingly suggest another solution than the one she's trying. Heal her heart, Lord, and give me guidance in the process. In Christ's name, amen.

Day 296

LIFTING WEIGHTS OF SIN

"Forgive, and you will be forgiven."

LUKE 6:37 NIV

Dear Lord, I am struggling to forgive. I don't want to; I want to hold on to my resentment and continue to look at it and pet it and admire it. Help me, Lord. Each time I do this, Lord—allow You to come into a situation and help me forgive—it feels like the hardest thing I have ever done. I lay my burden at the cross, and suddenly I feel lighter. But then after a few minutes, or hours or days, I walk over and pick it up again. How could You do this for billions of people, when I can't even forgive *one* person and have it stick? I am looking to You, Jesus. Help me carry my cross daily in forgiveness and follow You. Amen.

Day 297

STANDING UP STRAIGHT

Teach me to do thy will; for thou art my God: thy spirit is good; lead me into the land of uprightness.

PSALM 143:10 KJV

My burdens have been feeling extra heavy lately, Father. I am still walking along Your path, but maybe You've noticed my shoulders slumped, my head hung low. Gently remind me that I don't need to carry these burdens—that You are strong enough to carry all the weight of the world. I give You my worries and woes, Father. Help me to stand upright and follow the path of Your perfect will.

MENTORING

May [the aged women] teach the young women to be sober, to love their husbands, to love their children.

Titus 2:4 kjv

Dear God, the Bible tells older women to mentor younger women. That's an element missing from my life. Although my mom did a great job of passing along the life lessons she'd learned and we have a good relationship, I still need the insight and affirmation of an older woman. Lord, I need a trusted confidante, one who will help me succeed. I ask You to send someone like that my way in fulfillment of Your Word. And let me fill that role myself some-day when I have the required résumé. Amen.

Day 299

EVERLASTING WAYS

*See if there be any wicked way in me,
and lead me in the way everlasting.*

PSALM 139:24 KJV

You know, Lord God, how easily I hide selfishness inside my heart. But try as I might, I cannot hide it from You. Shine Your light on all my blind spots. Show me where I need to grow and change to be more like You. Bring true godly friends into my life who can help me in these areas. Place me in the path that will lead me to eternity.

Day 300

INSTRUCTIONS IN RIGHTEOUSNESS

*"But I tell you, love your enemies and pray
for those who persecute you, that you may
be children of your Father in heaven."*

MATTHEW 5:44–45 NIV

On the same note, Lord, I want to thank You for this verse in Matthew. When You tell us to pray for our enemies (or even those we're just annoyed with), it works. I quite literally can't hold on to my negative feelings about a person when I'm lifting them up to You. Your Word is powerful, and when I obey it, I feel Your power at work in me. When I feel crushed by the weight of unforgiveness, like I don't have a hope or a prayer, this verse offers me both: it gives me a specific prayer to pray and tells what will happen if I do. I want to be Your child. Thank You for showing me how. Amen.

Day 301

THE SAME OLD ME

*You have searched me, L*ORD*, and you know me.*

PSALM 139:1 NIV

Lord, today I come to You a bit discouraged. The traits I see in myself are ones I don't like. It seems I could do much more for You without some of the inherent flaws of my personality. So help me overcome my defects, or please use me in spite of them. Help me love myself, as imperfect as I am, and strive to be the best me I can be. I know You can find a way around my impediments and use me for Your glory just like You used Moses in spite of his speech problem. Amen.

Day 302

FUTURE GLORY

*For I reckon that the sufferings of this present
time are not worthy to be compared with
the glory which shall be revealed in us.*

ROMANS 8:18 KJV

When it comes down to it, God, it's not all about me.
I am guilty of being so selfish, self-centered, "me
focused" that I lose perspective of the big picture.
Father God, when pain surrounds me, give me a
glimpse of the glory that lies ahead. Help me regain a
proper sense of perspective. Show me where You want
me in Your will!

Day 303

ETERNAL

*For our light affliction, which is but for
a moment, worketh for us a far more
exceeding and eternal weight of glory.*

2 Corinthians 4:17 kjv

When I think about eternity, God, I realize that the time I spend on earth is pretty insignificant. But I still get so focused on my daily problems, Lord, that they seem insurmountable. Burdens and worries eat away at my joy, Lord. Instead, I choose to yield myself to whatever comes into my life and rely on Your power to get me through. Use my problems and troubles to transform me for eternity, I pray.

Day 304

FORGIVE

You are from God, little children, and have overcome them; because greater is He who is in you than he who is in the world.

1 JOHN 4:4 NASB

Forgive me, Lord, for harping on the same subject over and over. I am so slow to learn the lessons You are teaching. But You are patient and loving. . .and *long-suffering*. Thank You for not giving up on me as I learn to forgive others. I remember the first time You helped me win this battle. I remember being alone in the car and yelling, "I can't forgive him! I won't!" But You just kept insisting, quietly and firmly, *"Forgive."* And then I did. I forgave and felt Your joy flood my heart. And I was *stronger*. Help me remember this victory, Lord, and keep strengthening my muscles for the harder battles to come. Amen.

Day 305

NOT GOOD ENOUGH

*I praise you because I am fearfully
and wonderfully made.*

PSALM 139:14 NIV

Father, shopping for clothing at the mall makes me so insecure. The store windows are filled with posters of glamorous women in size 0 clothing. I feel I will never "measure up" to these airbrushed supermodels. Like every other twenty-first-century woman I know, I struggle with body image. Although these feelings of inferiority seem petty and a bit self-centered, they are so real sometimes that I get depressed. I know that isn't what You want for me. Help me with these feelings, and show me the way to triumph over them. In Christ's name, amen.

Day 306

BLESSED HOPE

*Looking for that blessed hope, and the
glorious appearing of the great God
and our Saviour Jesus Christ.*

TITUS 2:13 KJV

Some days, Father, I hold on to a single thread of hope.
But the hope You offer through Jesus Christ is real and
active, and even when it's wearing thin, it sustains me.
The hope I have in You, God, is for the future—but it
blesses me today. Fortify my hope so that I can share
it with other weary travelers in this world. Help me
direct them to the true source of hope.

Day 307

TIMELY WISDOM

For the LORD gives wisdom; from His mouth come knowledge and understanding.

PROVERBS 2:6 NKJV

Lord, I wasted my time this afternoon watching a movie. I needed to do other things, but I got caught up in the plot. Now I'm running behind in my schedule. Thank You, Lord, for giving writers and moviemakers the gifts necessary to craft moving stories, sometimes life-changing dramas. But help me to use my time more wisely so I can enjoy this pleasure sans guilt. And, Lord, help me to guard my mind carefully when I'm selecting what to watch. Amen.

Day 308

WHEN CHRIST APPEARS

*When Christ, who is our life, shall appear,
then shall ye also appear with him in glory.*

COLOSSIANS 3:4 KJV

Jesus, I look forward to Your return to earth. I'm so thankful that I am not on my own—that You are with me all the way. Thank You for the gift of Your Holy Spirit that lives in me and empowers me with the strength necessary to live for God. You are my life now, and You will take me with You into glory, where I will be made perfect.

Day 309

A BOWL OF RICE, PLEASE

But godliness with contentment is great gain.

1 TIMOTHY 6:6 KJV

Dear Father, there has never been a nation so blessed with *things* and opportunities and peace as this one. I don't know why You chose to let me live here rather than, say, Angola or Eritrea or Afghanistan, but *thank* You. Yet, we are a nation with so many wants, and I am no different. Where someone in another country might want enough rice to fill his belly, a quiet night's sleep, or a doctor to treat his infected leg, we want another outfit to stuff in a jam-packed closet, the newest techno-gadget, and a house with a pool. It will never be enough, Lord. Only You can fill the hole we try to fill with stuff. Thank You that I want for nothing except contentment. Amen.

Day 310

THE POWER OF WORDS

Death and life are in the power of the tongue: and they that love it shall eat the fruit thereof.

PROVERBS 18:21 KJV

Father, my mouth sometimes gets me into trouble. Please keep me aware of the things I say that aren't right. Let me back up and apologize if I've hurt anyone. Better yet, let me consider my words before I cast them out on the wind. Once spoken, they can never be recalled. Your written Word is living, brilliant, and powerful; Jesus is the embodiment of it—the Living Word. My spoken earthly words are weighty as well; they can minister life or death to those who hear. I ask You to remind me of this throughout the day. Amen.

Day 311

GOD'S THOUGHTS

*For I know the thoughts that I think toward
you, saith the LORD, thoughts of peace, and
not of evil, to give you an expected end.*

JEREMIAH 29:11 KJV

God, You know how easily my thoughts turn to worries
and fears. Teach me to think Your thoughts instead:
thoughts of peace and goodness that will lead me into
the future You have planned for me. Show me the steps
I should take to reach the abundant life You have in
store for me both here on earth and in eternity.

Day 312

THE PEBBLE

"You did not choose me, but I chose you and appointed you so that you might go and bear fruit—fruit that will last."

John 15:16 niv

Sometimes I feel like I have no influence, Lord. That nothing I think or do resonates much beyond the walls of this house. But You comfort and empower me with Your Word again. Thank You for reminding me that no matter what small circles we move in, we are all leaders to someone: a child, a wife, a younger brother, a boy flipping burgers in a fast-food joint, a shy new believer in church. I am a tiny pebble thrown into the sea, Lord, but my ripples will travel. Amen.

Day 313

BEFORE THE WORLD BEGAN

In hope of eternal life, which God, that cannot lie, promised before the world began.

TITUS 1:2 KJV

Think of it, Father! You are a God that cannot lie—there is no falsehood or deceit in You. Your promises are better than gold and they reach forward into eternity—and they reach backward, before the heavens and earth were made. There is no place in time's long arc where You are not, so why should I worry about past, present, or future? Hold me in Your hand today.

Day 314

GOD'S RICHES

*Oh, the depth of the riches both of the wisdom
and knowledge of God! How unsearchable are
His judgments and unfathomable His ways!*

ROMANS 11:33 NASB

When I start to worry about my life, Father, when I
start to feel as though You may not know what You're
doing—remind me that Your riches are far greater
than my needs. Give me a spirit of peace when I don't
understand the whys, secure in my faith that You are
doing a good work that will bring glory to Your name.

THE MISSING LINK

*Then God said, "Let there be light"; and there
was light. God saw that the light was good;
and God separated the light from the darkness.*

GENESIS 1:3–4 NASB

Dear Lord, sometimes I have to laugh at how hard
people work to explain life apart from a Creator.
They are desperate to throw their lot in with amoebas
in a primordial soup pot rather than with a loving,
creative God who might require something of them.
But I thank You that You did create the universe
out of nothing and us out of the dust of the earth.
You spoke light into existence. Not in a billion years
could we design a universe so complex, detailed, and
interlocking. Thank You for the amazing love that
keeps it all spinning. Amen.

Day 316

ALL GRACE

*The God of all grace, who hath called us unto
his eternal glory by Christ Jesus, after that ye
have suffered a while, make you perfect,
stablish, strengthen, settle you.*

1 PETER 5:10 KJV

I'm glad, God, that Your grace is so wide and great that
it can work even through this life's pain and suffering.
Give me the right amount of comfort to endure those
times of pain and suffering, and remind me that in
the end, I can count on You to make me perfect and
strong, settled in Your love forever.

Day 317

ABUNDANCE

[God] is able to do exceeding abundantly above all that we ask or think, according to the power that worketh in us.

EPHESIANS 3:20 KJV

Father, I often put limits on what is possible in my life—to my own detriment! Help me recall the miracles You've done in my life—the "God incidents" that have Your fingerprints all over them. Remind me to share these fantastic stories with others so they too might learn to see You at work in their lives. Give me Your eyes to see the endless power You have at work in me. May I expect Your abundance to fill my future.

Day 318

OBSIDIAN

*The LORD liveth; and blessed be my rock; and
exalted be the God of the rock of my salvation.*

2 SAMUEL 22:47 KJV

Lord, my house is full of the flu, but I praise You with
a kind of wide-eyed joy. I feel *patience* (where did
that come from?) thickening like a skin over the lava
of my usual anger, and I know that it can only come
from You. I walk gingerly, Lord, because I don't yet
trust myself. Will I fall through? Is it thick enough to
hold? But thank You for what You are slowly forming
beneath my feet: solid rock. Amen.

Day 319

NO SPIRIT OF FEAR

For God hath not given us the spirit of fear;
but of power, and of love, and of a sound mind.

2 TIMOTHY 1:7 KJV

Father, I deal with a phobia. It isn't anything life threatening, but it's embarrassing. I haven't told anyone, and I'm hoping I never have to. But I ask You now to help me; I don't want my phobia to keep me from living the life You've planned for me. Help me to bring this fear to You; show me that You are in control, that You are the security system in my life. I ask this in Jesus' name, amen.

Day 320

SHINING MORE AND MORE

The path of the just is as the shining light, that shineth more and more unto the perfect day.

PROVERBS 4:18 KJV

Father, when I am in vibrant fellowship with You, the path before me seems clearer and Your will seems more evident. Thank You for the light that shines brighter with each step I take. When the light seems dim or I'm not sure which way to go, bring me back into Your presence and lead me to Your holy Word. Thank You for never giving up on me, Father.

PACK NOTHING BUT FAITH

*Now faith is the assurance of things hoped
for, the conviction of things not seen.*

HEBREWS 11:1 NASB

Dear Lord, Your world is so beautiful and *large*.
Sometimes I sigh for all the places I will never see
before I die. Mount Everest flying its white cloud-flag
of spindrift. Greek islands floating in a wine-dark sea.
A blue morpho flickering through the black-green-
gold of the jungle. I miss them somehow, though I've
never seen them. But I know that nothing good will
be lost, and I am confident that in heaven, I will ache
for nothing left behind. I praise You for what *is* and for
what will be. Amen.

Day 322

FIXING MY THOUGHTS

Fix your thoughts on what is true, and honorable, and right, and pure, and lovely, and admirable.

PHILIPPIANS 4:8 NLT

God, today I'm having a pity party. My thoughts are so focused on earthly things that I am having trouble looking up. I could mope around here all day, but I guess it's time for the music to stop and the party to end. Lord, You can't work through me when I'm feeling sorry for myself. Forgive me for my pettiness, and let me respond to life with maturity. Help me focus on good, praiseworthy things. In Christ's name, amen.

Day 323

LIKE JESUS

*Beloved, now are we the sons of God, and it
doth not yet appear what we shall be: but we
know that, when he shall appear, we shall
be like him; for we shall see him as he is.*

1 JOHN 3:2 KJV

God, You promise that You're not done with me
yet. In fact, I won't be finished until You come again
to the earth and take me home with You. It doesn't
really matter what my future holds, God, so long as
one day I will be like Jesus.

Day 324

FACE-TO-FACE

For now we see through a glass, darkly;
but then face to face: now I know in part;
but then shall I know even as also I am known.

1 CORINTHIANS 13:12 KJV

You know that I can't see You clearly, Father. You know I don't really understand You, even when I am seeking You every day. I'm grateful, though, that I expect to see You face-to-face—and that on that day, I will finally truly know You even more intimately and personally than now. What an awe-inspiring promise!

Day 325

FLU SEASON

The LORD will strengthen him on his bed of illness; You will sustain him on his sickbed.

PSALM 41:3 NKJV

Now the flu's got me too, Lord, and I feel like I'm hanging on by the skin of my teeth, whatever that means. But You use everything to draw us closer to You, and even in this I can see You. Though I feel terrible right now, this virus will run its course; in a day or two I'll feel well again. But I won't *really* be well because I am also infected with another terrible disease, Lord, which will only be healed in glory: sin. I praise You, Comforter, Healer, Sustainer, for what You are doing right now in my body and what You *will* do when I see You face-to-face. Amen.

Day 326

FADELESS BEAUTY

The unfading beauty of a gentle and quiet spirit, which is so precious to God.

1 PETER 3:4 NLT

Dear God, I'm getting older. That's not news to You, I know. You've seen my journey from day one. But now my body is revolting, and my hormones are rebelling. I don't like looking in the mirror because it shocks me to see lines on my face. Inside I don't feel old, but my body doesn't agree. Still, Lord, help me remember that my identity in You is changeless, and my beauty in You is fadeless. The magazines may say differently, but I know that, in Your sight, I have a loveliness that time can't touch. Amen.

Day 327

GLORY TO GLORY

But we all, with open face beholding as in a glass the glory of the Lord, are changed into the same image from glory to glory, even as by the Spirit of the Lord.

2 CORINTHIANS 3:18 KJV

You have given me glory in this world, God. You have given me splendor and light. You have created my very essence so that it shines. And as I keep my eyes on You, You are creating within me even greater glory. May Your Spirit work in my heart, God, so that I am transformed into Your image.

Day 328

UNBLEMISHED

And He who sits on the throne said,
"Behold, I am making all things new."

REVELATION 21:5 NASB

Lord, I praise You today for babies, for the gift of new life, and the new life I have in You. I marvel at the perfect, round cheeks of my baby, his skin so smooth and firm and kissable. His silky hair lighter than air, his wide, bright eyes. When he smiles, his face is all joy. Do You see me this way, Lord? Do I bring You this much joy? Sometimes I have a hard time believing that I—with my sags and bags and scars—am fearfully and wonderfully made. But I trust Your promises and Your love. I trust the blood of Jesus that has washed me into new life. Amen.

Day 329

STRENGTH TO STRENGTH

They go from strength to strength.

PSALM 84:7 KJV

You know the strength I need to face today, Lord. You know the strength I'll need for tomorrow, for next week, for next year. You know what I'll need to face each of the challenges that lie ahead in my life. You know the day of my death, and You know exactly what I'll need on that day too. So I need not worry about anything. You will lead me from strength to strength, like jumping from stone to stone across a river.

Day 330

WHAT WILL BE

*The earth will be full of the knowledge of
the LORD as the waters cover the sea.*

ISAIAH 11:9 NASB

Dear Father, the more I know about Your creation, the more I marvel at the mind that conceived it. The more I marvel at You. Your creation is irreducibly complex, multifaceted, and breathtakingly beautiful whether viewed from a satellite or in a microscope. And we are only just beginning *to begin* to fathom its mysteries. I praise You for the spirit of inquiry that You fashioned in us along with the breath of life. I praise You that You are *knowable*. And I praise You for the day when we will know You fully. Amen.

Day 331

COVETING

Let your conduct be without covetousness.

HEBREWS 13:5 NKJV

God, it's so easy to break the tenth commandment: do not covet (see Exodus 20:17). Coveting is a way of life for many in our world. But You say we shouldn't compare ourselves with the "Joneses" nor envy them and what they have. Whatever You've given me is to be enjoyed and received, not held up for inspection. Teach me a deeper gratefulness for Your blessings. In Jesus' name, amen.

Day 332

WITH JESUS

Father, I will that they also, whom thou hast given me, be with me where I am; that they may behold my glory, which thou hast given me.

JOHN 17:24 KJV

God, as much as I may wish I knew what the future holds, only You know what will happen. Instead of worrying about things that I cannot control, I want to simply follow You into tomorrow and into eternity. The truth is, I don't really care where You lead me. . .so long as Jesus is there too.

Day 333

JOY

*For ye shall go out with joy, and be led forth
with peace: the mountains and the hills shall
break forth before you into singing, and all
the trees of the field shall clap their hands.*

ISAIAH 55:12 KJV

Some days, Lord, things are going so well that it feels
like all of creation is singing Your praises, and I join
with them. Other days, even when creation sings, I don't
feel like praising. Thank You, Lord, for the reminder
from the mountains and trees that no matter what
today brings, You promise me joy. Help me live out
Your joy every day.

Day 334

I WILL LIFT UP MINE EYES

*Let the rivers clap their hands, let the
mountains sing together for joy.*

PSALM 98:8 NIV

Lord, I praise You for mountains. I praise You for the old, rolling backs of the Appalachians. I praise You for the sharp, unworn spires of the Himalayas. I praise You for snowcapped peaks and glacier-grooved summits and the way mountains train my eyes *upward*. Lord, I so often fix my eyes on the pebbles at my feet, on the trivialities that trip me and dog my path. Give me Your eyes, Lord. Give me the long view. Thank You for this trail I am on, Lord, the sights along the way, and the vista that awaits at the end. Amen.

Day 335

LET IT BE

*And Mary said, Behold the handmaid of the
Lord; be it unto me according to thy word.*

LUKE 1:38 KJV

Lord, help me follow Mary's example when she found
out that she was pregnant with the Son of God. Her
world was rocked, God! What a scandal! A good Jewish
girl pregnant before she was married? Unthinkable!
But she accepted the news and surrendered her life and
her body to Your will. Help me accept Your Word, no
matter what it says to me, and surrender myself to it.

RIGHT MOTIVES

Ye ask, and receive not, because ye ask amiss,
that ye may consume it upon your lusts.

JAMES 4:3 KJV

God, I admit that sometimes I am guilty of treating my prayers as a wish list to a Santa-God. Or maybe I treat You as though You were a vending machine— if I say the right words in the right order, I'll get what I want. If I'm honest, I know that selfishness and greed may slip into a request here or there. Today I ask that You show me when my prayers are corrupted by selfish desires. Give me pure motives, a pure heart, and a clear conscience.

GOLDEN WORDS NEEDED

*A word fitly spoken is like apples
of gold in settings of silver.*

PROVERBS 25:11 NKJV

Heavenly Father, today I need affirming words. You know that words are important to me as a woman. You also know that I struggle with self-worth. The other people in my world don't always meet my need to be affirmed verbally, and I can't expect them to fill every void in my life. So, Lord, let me look to and in Your Word to find the love and encouragement I need. In Jesus' name, amen.

Day 338

OVERTAKEN

*But My words and My statutes, which I commanded
My servants the prophets, did they not overtake
and take hold of your fathers? So they repented.*

ZECHARIAH 1:6 AMPC

So often, Lord, when I imagine witnessing to someone, I think I have to have every argument and counterargument planned out twelve moves in advance, like it's a chess game. I think of potential questions, and if I don't have perfect answers for them, that's enough to keep me from opening my mouth at all. But Your Word is so clear: *we* do not convert the lost. The Gospel is *alive*. It converts. It overtakes. Lord, I trust Your Word and its mighty power to do what I cannot. Amen.

Day 339

CONFIDENCE

And this is the confidence that we have in him, that, if we ask any thing according to his will, he heareth us.

1 JOHN 5:14 KJV

As I pray, Lord, I rest in the confidence that You are always listening and that You understand the thoughts behind my prayers, even when I cannot. I am never speaking into empty air! Thank You for the confidence I also experience through the power of Your Holy Spirit that lives inside my heart. With You on my side, I can accomplish much for Your kingdom!

THE TRUTH

Jesus saith unto him, I am the way, the truth, and the life: no man cometh unto the Father, but by me.

JOHN 14:6 KJV

When I pray to You, God, I pray in Your Son's name. He is the Way, He is the Truth, and He will show me the way to You so that I can live the life that You intend for me. Help me to not be distracted by other false paths that may seem attractive or easier. Make my journey one that invites others to follow me just as I follow Christ.

Day 341

A JOYFUL NOISE

Shout joyfully to the LORD, all the earth;
break forth in song, rejoice, and sing praises.

PSALM 98:4 NKJV

Dear God, I thank You for music. For the music of rain on rooftops and wind in bare branches. For the splash of water over stones. For little children shouting a hymn at the top of their lungs. For a Bach organ concerto. Lord, Your creation praises You all the time with every breath and in every moment. Thank You for letting me join in this eternal song of praise. Hallelujah! Worthy is the Lamb who was slain!

Day 342

UNITED IN PRAYER

I say unto you, That if two of you shall agree on earth as touching any thing that they shall ask, it shall be done for them of my Father which is in heaven.

MATTHEW 18:19 KJV

Thank You, Lord, for others who share my faith in You. Thank You for the privilege of praying with them, for worshipping with them, for working together to build Your kingdom. Thank You that when we pray together, You hear us, and that when we gather together, You are there with us. Help us to be the living, breathing, and active body of Christ that we are meant to be.

Day 343

DRY MOUTH

We also believe and therefore speak.

2 Corinthians 4:13 nkjv

Lord, You can use anyone to spread the Good News. You can use invalids, the elderly, fishermen, the mentally challenged, paupers, rich men, tax collectors, children, even me. Thank You that You don't require me to know everything or have every answer. You don't require me to be well traveled or well dressed. You don't require a seminary degree. You don't require me to be anything but saved by the blood of Jesus The only requirement for evangelism is that I believe and speak. Lord, I believe. Now open my mouth.

Day 344

ABIDING

If ye abide in me, and my words abide in you, ye shall ask what ye will, and it shall be done unto you.

JOHN 15:7 KJV

Father, help me abide in You as I pray—not quickly spitting out my requests and then dwelling on my worries and woes. Keep my thoughts focused on You as I wait for Your answers to my prayers, no matter how soon You answer them. Keep me close, and allow me to abide in You as You ultimately answer my requests and give me the peace of knowing that You work all things for good.

Day 345

WAVERING HEARTS

Let him ask in faith, nothing wavering.
For he that wavereth is like a wave of the
sea driven with the wind and tossed.

JAMES 1:6 KJV

You know how easily my heart wavers and wobbles, Lord. I'm like a boat that's out in open water, the world's woes tossing me around like high waves. Take the helm of my boat, I pray. And then after I've given over control of the boat, quiet the wind and waves. Help me pray with faith's absolute calm, knowing that You have already ordained the outcome and that You have my best interest at heart.

TO A GOD WHO MADE GIRAFFES

Then our mouth was filled with laughter
and our tongue with joyful shouting.

PSALM 126:2 NASB

Dear Lord, I praise You for laughter. Tonight I laughed until my sides ached, and it was *good*. Now I feel cleansed and emptied of distress and strangely content. Thank You for being a God whose miracles bring laughter: Sarah with the news of her improbable baby, Lazarus raised to life, and the disciples with their ridiculous catch of fish. I can imagine You standing there, Lord, and laughing until the tears came with the people You love. Thank You for giraffes and hedgehogs and zebras and penguins, and how You long to astonish us with joy. Amen.

Day 347

POISE

Like a gold ring in a pig's snout is a beautiful woman who shows no discretion.

PROVERBS 11:22 NIV

Heavenly Father, I need poise—that kind of gracious manner and behavior that characterized women of past generations. It seems to be disdained in my culture. Women now are expected and encouraged to be free spirits—unrestricted by convention and decorum. But I cringe when I observe women using crude language, slouching in their seats, and adopting careless ways of walking and eating. I don't want to seem prissy and uppity, but I do want to guard against being too informal. Help me develop the traits that portray womanhood as the gentle, beautiful, fascinating gender You designed. Amen.

Day 348

ANYTHING!

*For verily I say unto you, that whosoever shall say
unto this mountain, Be thou removed, and be thou
cast into the sea; and shall not doubt in his heart,
but shall believe that those things which he saith shall
come to pass; he shall have whatsoever he saith.*

MARK 11:23 KJV

I don't want to throw any mountains into the ocean,
God—and it's hard for me to believe that Jesus really
meant what He said here. Show me the truth of His
words. Teach me to pray according to Your will.

Day 349

POWER

*The effectual fervent prayer of a
righteous man availeth much.*

JAMES 5:16 KJV

Sometimes I say, "The only thing I can do now is pray."
I mean that I've done everything I could think to do,
and now as a last resort, I'll fall back on prayer. Forgive
me, Father, for trusting in things that are not from You
and for setting my mind on worldly things. Remind
me that prayer is never the last resort and that You
are faithful in hearing it. Teach me to see the power
that prayer can unleash in the world.

Day 350

WELL BEGUN IS HALF DONE

Now faith is the substance of things hoped for, the evidence of things not seen.

HEBREWS 11:1 NKJV

Dear God, there is something You've asked me to do that I've been putting off for a long time. You haven't forgotten—though *I've* certainly tried to. You keep gently reminding and prodding me to obey. Tonight, as I was walking and pondering this in the darkness between streetlights, I was filled with a cheerful certainty that by the next day, I would have begun. And this wasn't wishful thinking, was it, Lord? It was *faith*. Thank You for believing in what is not yet visible in me and allowing me to do the same. Amen.

Day 351

LESSONS IN TRUST

I have put my trust in the Lord God,
that I may declare all Your works.

PSALM 73:28 NKJV

Heavenly Father, teach me to trust. I know it's an area of weakness for me. In spite of the fact that I know Your character and Your track record, I find it so difficult to relinquish to You the important areas of life. Oh I say that I will, and I do put forth effort to rely on You, but we both know that, in my heart, I find it hard to let You handle everything. So take my hand, Lord, and teach me to trust. You're the Master; I am forever Your student. In Christ's name, amen.

Day 352

IN ALL MY WAYS

In all thy ways acknowledge him,
and he shall direct thy paths.

<small>PROVERBS 3:6 KJV</small>

God, I claim Your presence in each aspect of my life. Thank You for Your steadfast love and abounding grace. I honor You alone with my successes and acknowledge Your guiding hand on my life. Help me set my eyes only on You. Teach me what it is to trust You with all my heart and to not lean on my own wisdom or understanding. May my heart always seek to bring glory to Your name, and may my prayers always reflect this reality.

WILLING MIND

*Know thou the God of thy father, and serve
him with a perfect heart and with a willing
mind: for the LORD searcheth all hearts, and
understandeth all the imaginations of the thoughts:
if thou seek him, he will be found of thee.*

1 CHRONICLES 28:9 KJV

Make my mind willing, Lord. Help me trust that Your
plans for me are better than the plans I have for myself.
Place Your desires in my heart, that I may be able to
walk fully in Your will for my life. Help me agree with
Your ways for my life. I seek You who understands me
completely.

THE GIVER

*You open your hand and satisfy the
desires of every living thing.*

PSALM 145:16 NIV

Lord, I've never been hungry; I've never been naked;
I've never been without shelter. You have been a faithful
provider of the things You know I need. Thank You
for my parents, who provided for me from birth to age
twenty-three. And thank You for my husband, who has
so faithfully provided for me in the years since then.
Thank You, Lord, for providing for me through their
generosity and hard work. It's humbling to realize that
I've never been completely self-sufficient at any point in
my life, yet there is a lesson in that too. We are paupers
by nature: *all* is from You. I praise my open-handed
God! Amen.

Day 355

PERFECT HEART

*Let your heart therefore be perfect with the
LORD our God, to walk in his statutes, and to
keep his commandments, as at this day.*

1 KINGS 8:61 KJV

You know I can never achieve perfection on my own,
Lord God. But I surrender my heart to You absolutely.
Keep my heart and mind from wandering and allow
me to remain true only to You. I thank You for Your
never-ending grace that sustains my life and that You
never leave me or forsake me. Through my prayer, I
commit myself totally to You and Your law for my life.

Day 356

DIVINE GUIDANCE

*If any of you lacks wisdom, you should ask
God, who gives generously to all without
finding fault, and it will be given to you.*

JAMES 1:5 NIV

Dear Lord, it's so hard sometimes to know what Your will is. You don't write specific instructions in the sky nor emblazon them on a marquee. So how can I know exactly what You want me to do? How can I keep from making a big mistake? How can I proceed with this decision? I ask today that You would give me wisdom, send me guidance as I seek Your will. Through a person, a thought, a scripture, let me sense Your leading for this situation. I want my life to honor Your plan for me. In Christ's name, amen.

Day 357

CELEBRATION

They celebrate your abundant goodness
and joyfully sing of your righteousness.

PSALM 145:7 NIV

Dear Father, so many people who don't know You see You as a heavenly killjoy, stopping them from doing really fun things that would bring them great enjoyment. But we know You better! Thank You that You do not delight in denial; You delight in saying yes to Your people. But more importantly, You delight in *us* and what is for our ultimate good, not just fun for a moment. And You are planning the ultimate party—one that will last forever. I can't wait to join the celebration! Amen.

Day 358

WILLING

I know also, my God, that thou triest
the heart, and hast pleasure in uprightness.
As for me, in the uprightness of mine heart
I have willingly offered all these things.

1 CHRONICLES 29:17 KJV

I give You, God, everything I have to offer, willingly and gladly. I know that everything I have You have provided and entrusted to me. Give me a whole heart to follow after You and keep Your commandments. Keep forever in my heart Your purposes and thoughts. Show me anything I am holding back. I want You to have it all.

Day 359

DEEP SURRENDER

But now, O Lord, You are our Father;
we are the clay, and You our potter;
and all we are the work of Your hand.

ISAIAH 64:8 NKJV

Lord, I need to surrender to You. You've shown me an area of my life that I've been trying to rule. I know You need the keys to every room in my heart, and so here I am, bringing this one to You. *Surrender* means I give You permission to change, clean out, and add things. Waving the white flag isn't really easy, but it's the way to true joy. Thank You for showing me that. Amen.

Day 360

TRUTHFUL HEART

Lord, who shall abide in thy tabernacle?
who shall dwell in thy holy hill? He that
walketh uprightly, and worketh righteousness,
and speaketh the truth in his heart.

PSALM 15:1–2 KJV

Lord, sometimes I lie to myself. Sometimes I try to lie to You. But You know me. You know my thoughts before I think them. Reveal to me Your truth so that my prayers may be true, righteous, and upright. Show me how to live a blameless life.

Day 361

HIS WORK

For the eyes of the Lord are on the righteous
and his ears are attentive to their prayer.

1 PETER 3:12 NIV

God, I am amazed that You never tire of listening to me. *I* get tired of listening to me, Lord! The same fears, the same complaints, the same problems, the same confusions—year after year. Yet, even I see progress, and I praise You. I am not who I was, and I know it's all because of You. Thank You for how You continue to work in me: so faithfully, patiently, lovingly. You are the Potter; I am the grateful clay in Your hands. Amen.

Day 362

ONE MIND

That ye may with one mind and one mouth glorify God, even the Father of our Lord Jesus Christ.

ROMANS 15:6 KJV

Unite me in prayer with others, Father God. Let no division come between us as we talk with You. Give me patience in dealing with people who aren't exactly like me and can be trying; remind me that patience will build up Your church. Forgive me for any gossip or malicious words I've spoken against my brothers and sisters, and give me a heart that longs for their good. Bring to my mind ways I can show love that will bring more glory to You.

Day 363

BELIEVING

Be not faithless, but believing.

JOHN 20:27 KJV

I believe in You, Jesus. I believe in Your power and wisdom and love. I believe that Your atoning work on the cross has washed me of all my unrighteousness and that through it, I stand in perfect righteousness before God. Take my life—all my words and deeds—and use them for Your glory. Teach me to trust You, not requiring proof as Thomas did but believing You at Your Word alone. Thank You that Your Word is truth and brings life to me and to those around me.

Day 364

ENDURANCE REQUIRED

*Let us run with endurance the
race that is set before us.*

HEBREWS 12:1 NKJV

I'm finding, Lord, that the Christian life is one that
requires endurance. It isn't enough to start well. So
let me patiently and steadily move down the road to
Christlikeness. I know difficulties will come; I've faced
some already. It reminds me of the words of the second
verse of "Amazing Grace": "Through many dangers,
toils, and snares, I have already come. 'Tis grace that
brought me safe thus far, and grace will lead me home."
In Your name, amen.

Day 365

THE GRAND TIMELINE

He has made everything beautiful in its time. He has also set eternity in the human heart; yet no one can fathom what God has done from beginning to end.

ECCLESIASTES 3:11 NIV

Lord, thank You for the grand story of history, which is really *Your* story. I see exploration, discovery, and war all muddled together, repeating, and leading *where?* But You had the end in mind from the beginning. I know I can trust that You are leading us to an end and to a good place. And I praise You for the amazing grace that has allowed my story to be a small part of the story You are telling. Amen.

Scripture Index

READ THROUGH THE BIBLE IN A YEAR

1-Jan	Gen. 1-2	Matt. 1	Ps. 1
2-Jan	Gen. 3-4	Matt. 2	Ps. 2
3-Jan	Gen. 5-7	Matt. 3	Ps. 3
4-Jan	Gen. 8-10	Matt. 4	Ps. 4
5-Jan	Gen. 11-13	Matt. 5:1-20	Ps. 5
6-Jan	Gen. 14-16	Matt. 5:21-48	Ps. 6
7-Jan	Gen. 17-18	Matt. 6:1-18	Ps. 7
8-Jan	Gen. 19-20	Matt. 6:19-34	Ps. 8
9-Jan	Gen. 21-23	Matt. 7:1-11	Ps. 9:1-8
10-Jan	Gen. 24	Matt. 7:12-29	Ps. 9:9-20
11-Jan	Gen. 25-26	Matt. 8:1-17	Ps. 10:1-11
12-Jan	Gen. 27:1-28:9	Matt. 8:18-34	Ps. 10:12-18
13-Jan	Gen. 28:10-29:35	Matt. 9	Ps. 11
14-Jan	Gen. 30:1-31:21	Matt. 10:1-15	Ps. 12
15-Jan	Gen. 31:22-32:21	Matt. 10:16-36	Ps. 13
16-Jan	Gen. 32:22-34:31	Matt. 10:37-11:6	Ps. 14
17-Jan	Gen. 35-36	Matt. 11:7-24	Ps. 15
18-Jan	Gen. 37-38	Matt. 11:25-30	Ps. 16
19-Jan	Gen. 39-40	Matt. 12:1-29	Ps. 17
20-Jan	Gen. 41	Matt. 12:30-50	Ps. 18:1-15
21-Jan	Gen. 42-43	Matt. 13:1-9	Ps. 18:16-29
22-Jan	Gen. 44-45	Matt. 13:10-23	Ps. 18:30-50
23-Jan	Gen. 46:1-47:26	Matt. 13:24-43	Ps. 19
24-Jan	Gen. 47:27-49:28	Matt. 13:44-58	Ps. 20
25-Jan	Gen. 49:29-Exod. 1:22	Matt. 14	Ps. 21
26-Jan	Exod. 2-3	Matt. 15:1-28	Ps. 22:1-21
27-Jan	Exod. 4:1-5:21	Matt. 15:29-16:12	Ps. 22:22-31
28-Jan	Exod. 5:22-7:24	Matt. 16:13-28	Ps. 23
29-Jan	Exod. 7:25-9:35	Matt. 17:1-9	Ps. 24
30-Jan	Exod. 10-11	Matt. 17:10-27	Ps. 25
31-Jan	Exod. 12	Matt. 18:1-20	Ps. 26
1-Feb	Exod. 13-14	Matt. 18:21-35	Ps. 27
2-Feb	Exod. 15-16	Matt. 19:1-15	Ps. 28
3-Feb	Exod. 17-19	Matt. 19:16-30	Ps. 29
4-Feb	Exod. 20-21	Matt. 20:1-19	Ps. 30
5-Feb	Exod. 22-23	Matt. 20:20-34	Ps. 31:1-8
6-Feb	Exod. 24-25	Matt. 21:1-27	Ps. 31:9-18
7-Feb	Exod 26-27	Matt. 21:28-46	Ps. 31:19-24
8-Feb	Exod. 28	Matt. 22	Ps. 32
9-Feb	Exod. 29	Matt. 23:1-36	Ps. 33:1-12
10-Feb	Exod. 30-31	Matt. 23:37-24:28	Ps. 33:13-22
11-Feb	Exod. 32-33	Matt. 24:29-51	Ps. 34:1-7
12-Feb	Exod. 34:1-35:29	Matt. 25:1-13	Ps. 34:8-22

13-Feb	Exod. 35:30-37:29	Matt. 25:14-30	Ps. 35:1-8
14-Feb	Exod. 38-39	Matt. 25:31-46	Ps. 35:9-17
15-Feb	Exod. 40	Matt. 26:1-35	Ps. 35:18-28
16-Feb	Lev. 1-3	Matt. 26:36-68	Ps. 36:1-6
17-Feb	Lev. 4:1-5:13	Matt. 26:69-27:26	Ps. 36:7-12
18-Feb	Lev. 5:14 -7:21	Matt. 27:27-50	Ps. 37:1-6
19-Feb	Lev. 7:22-8:36	Matt. 27:51-66	Ps. 37:7-26
20-Feb	Lev. 9-10	Matt. 28	Ps. 37:27-40
21-Feb	Lev. 11-12	Mark 1:1-28	Ps. 38
22-Feb	Lev. 13	Mark 1:29-39	Ps. 39
23-Feb	Lev. 14	Mark 1:40-2:12	Ps. 40:1-8
24-Feb	Lev. 15	Mark 2:13-3:35	Ps. 40:9-17
25-Feb	Lev. 16-17	Mark 4:1-20	Ps. 41:1-4
26-Feb	Lev. 18-19	Mark 4:21-41	Ps. 41:5-13
27-Feb	Lev. 20	Mark 5	Ps. 42-43
28-Feb	Lev. 21-22	Mark 6:1-13	Ps. 44
1-Mar	Lev. 23-24	Mark 6:14-29	Ps. 45:1-5
2-Mar	Lev. 25	Mark 6:30-56	Ps. 45:6-12
3-Mar	Lev. 26	Mark 7	Ps. 45:13-17
4-Mar	Lev. 27	Mark 8	Ps. 46
5-Mar	Num. 1-2	Mark 9:1-13	Ps. 47
6-Mar	Num. 3	Mark 9:14-50	Ps. 48:1-8
7-Mar	Num. 4	Mark 10:1-34	Ps. 48:9-14
8-Mar	Num. 5:1-6:21	Mark 10:35-52	Ps. 49:1-9
9-Mar	Num. 6:22-7:47	Mark 11	Ps. 49:10-20
10-Mar	Num. 7:48-8:4	Mark 12:1-27	Ps. 50:1-15
11-Mar	Num. 8:5-9:23	Mark 12:28-44	Ps. 50:16-23
12-Mar	Num. 10-11	Mark 13:1-8	Ps. 51:1-9
13-Mar	Num. 12-13	Mark 13:9-37	Ps. 51:10-19
14-Mar	Num. 14	Mark 14:1-31	Ps. 52
15-Mar	Num. 15	Mark 14:32-72	Ps. 53
16-Mar	Num. 16	Mark 15:1-32	Ps. 54
17-Mar	Num. 17-18	Mark 15:33-47	Ps. 55
18-Mar	Num. 19-20	Mark 16	Ps. 56:1-7
19-Mar	Num. 21:1-22:20	Luke 1:1-25	Ps. 56:8-13
20-Mar	Num. 22:21-23:30	Luke 1:26-56	Ps. 57
21-Mar	Num. 24-25	Luke 1:57-2:20	Ps. 58
22-Mar	Num. 26:1-27:11	Luke 2:21-38	Ps. 59:1-8
23-Mar	Num. 27:12-29:11	Luke 2:39-52	Ps. 59:9-17
24-Mar	Num. 29:12-30:16	Luke 3	Ps. 60:1-5
25-Mar	Num. 31	Luke 4	Ps. 60:6-12
26-Mar	Num. 32-33	Luke 5:1-16	Ps. 61
27-Mar	Num. 34-36	Luke 5:17-32	Ps. 62:1-6
28-Mar	Deut. 1:1-2:25	Luke 5:33-6:11	Ps. 62:7-12

29-Mar	Deut. 2:26-4:14	Luke 6:12-35	Ps. 63:1-5
30-Mar	Deut. 4:15-5:22	Luke 6:36-49	Ps. 63:6-11
31-Mar	Deut. 5:23-7:26	Luke 7:1-17	Ps. 64:1-5
1-Apr	Deut. 8-9	Luke 7:18-35	Ps. 64:6-10
2-Apr	Deut. 10-11	Luke 7:36-8:3	Ps. 65:1-8
3-Apr	Deut. 12-13	Luke 8:4-21	Ps. 65:9-13
4-Apr	Deut. 14:1-16:8	Luke 8:22-39	Ps. 66:1-7
5-Apr	Deut. 16:9-18:22	Luke 8:40-56	Ps. 66:8-15
6-Apr	Deut. 19:1-21:9	Luke 9:1-22	Ps. 66:16-20
7-Apr	Deut. 21:10-23:8	Luke 9:23-42	Ps. 67
8-Apr	Deut. 23:9-25:19	Luke 9:43-62	Ps. 68:1-6
9-Apr	Deut. 26:1-28:14	Luke 10:1-20	Ps. 68:7-14
10-Apr	Deut. 28:15-68	Luke 10:21-37	Ps. 68:15-19
11-Apr	Deut. 29-30	Luke 10:38-11:23	Ps. 68:20-27
12-Apr	Deut. 31:1-32:22	Luke 11:24-36	Ps. 68:28-35
13-Apr	Deut. 32:23-33:29	Luke 11:37-54	Ps. 69:1-9
14-Apr	Deut. 34-Josh. 2	Luke 12:1-15	Ps. 69:10-17
15-Apr	Josh. 3:1-5:12	Luke 12:16-40	Ps. 69:18-28
16-Apr	Josh. 5:13-7:26	Luke 12:41-48	Ps. 69:29-36
17-Apr	Josh. 8-9	Luke 12:49-59	Ps. 70
18-Apr	Josh. 10:1-11:15	Luke 13:1-21	Ps. 71:1-6
19-Apr	Josh. 11:16-13:33	Luke 13:22-35	Ps. 71:7-16
20-Apr	Josh. 14-16	Luke 14:1-15	Ps. 71:17-21
21-Apr	Josh. 17:1-19:16	Luke 14:16-35	Ps. 71:22-24
22-Apr	Josh. 19:17-21:42	Luke 15:1-10	Ps. 72:1-11
23-Apr	Josh. 21:43-22:34	Luke 15:11-32	Ps. 72:12-20
24-Apr	Josh. 23-24	Luke 16:1-18	Ps. 73:1-9
25-Apr	Judg. 1-2	Luke 16:19-17:10	Ps. 73:10-20
26-Apr	Judg. 3-4	Luke 17:11-37	Ps. 73:21-28
27-Apr	Judg. 5:1-6:24	Luke 18:1-17	Ps. 74:1-3
28-Apr	Judg. 6:25-7:25	Luke 18:18-43	Ps. 74:4-11
29-Apr	Judg. 8:1-9:23	Luke 19:1-28	Ps. 74:12-17
30-Apr	Judg. 9:24-10:18	Luke 19:29-48	Ps. 74:18-23
1-May	Judg. 11:1-12:7	Luke 20:1-26	Ps. 75:1-7
2-May	Judg. 12:8-14:20	Luke 20:27-47	Ps. 75:8-10
3-May	Judg. 15-16	Luke 21:1-19	Ps. 76:1-7
4-May	Judg. 17-18	Luke 21:20-22:6	Ps. 76:8-12
5-May	Judg. 19:1-20:23	Luke 22:7-30	Ps. 77:1-11
6-May	Judg. 20:24-21:25	Luke 22:31-54	Ps. 77:12-20
7-May	Ruth 1-2	Luke 22:55-23:25	Ps. 78:1-4
8-May	Ruth 3-4	Luke 23:26-24:12	Ps. 78:5-8
9-May	1 Sam. 1:1-2:21	Luke 24:13-53	Ps. 78:9-16
10-May	1 Sam. 2:22-4:22	John 1:1-28	Ps. 78:17-24
11-May	1 Sam. 5-7	John 1:29-51	Ps. 78:25-33

12-May	1 Sam. 8:1-9:26	John 2	Ps. 78:34-41
13-May	1 Sam. 9:27-11:15	John 3:1-22	Ps. 78:42-55
14-May	1 Sam. 12-13	John 3:23-4:10	Ps. 78:56-66
15-May	1 Sam. 14	John 4:11-38	Ps. 78:67-72
16-May	1 Sam. 15-16	John 4:39-54	Ps. 79:1-7
17-May	1 Sam. 17	John 5:1-24	Ps. 79:8-13
18-May	1 Sam. 18-19	John 5:25-47	Ps. 80:1-7
19-May	1 Sam. 20-21	John 6:1-21	Ps. 80:8-19
20-May	1 Sam. 22-23	John 6:22-42	Ps. 81:1-10
21-May	1 Sam. 24:1-25:31	John 6:43-71	Ps. 81:11-16
22-May	1 Sam. 25:32-27:12	John 7:1-24	Ps. 82
23-May	1 Sam. 28-29	John 7:25-8:11	Ps. 83
24-May	1 Sam. 30-31	John 8:12-47	Ps. 84:1-4
25-May	2 Sam. 1-2	John 8:48-9:12	Ps. 84:5-12
26-May	2 Sam. 3-4	John 9:13-34	Ps. 85:1-7
27-May	2 Sam. 5:1-7:17	John 9:35-10:10	Ps. 85:8-13
28-May	2 Sam. 7:18-10:19	John 10:11-30	Ps. 86:1-10
29-May	2 Sam. 11:1-12:25	John 10:31-11:16	Ps. 86:11-17
30-May	2 Sam. 12:26-13:39	John 11:17-54	Ps. 87
31-May	2 Sam. 14:1-15:12	John 11:55-12:19	Ps. 88:1-9
1-Jun	2 Sam. 15:13-16:23	John 12:20-43	Ps. 88:10-18
2-Jun	2 Sam. 17:1-18:18	John 12:44-13:20	Ps. 89:1-6
3-Jun	2 Sam. 18:19-19:39	John 13:21-38	Ps. 89:7-13
4-Jun	2 Sam. 19:40-21:22	John 14:1-17	Ps. 89:14-18
5-Jun	2 Sam. 22:1-23:7	John 14:18-15:27	Ps. 89:19-29
6-Jun	2 Sam. 23:8-24:25	John 16:1-22	Ps. 89:30-37
7-Jun	1 Kings 1	John 16:23-17:5	Ps. 89:38-52
8-Jun	1 Kings 2	John 17:6-26	Ps. 90:1-12
9-Jun	1 Kings 3-4	John 18:1-27	Ps. 90:13-17
10-Jun	1 Kings 5-6	John 18:28-19:5	Ps. 91:1-10
11-Jun	1 Kings 7	John 19:6-25a	Ps. 91:11-16
12-Jun	1 Kings 8:1-53	John 19:25b-42	Ps. 92:1-9
13-Jun	1 Kings 8:54-10:13	John 20:1-18	Ps. 92:10-15
14-Jun	1 Kings 10:14-11:43	John 20:19-31	Ps. 93
15-Jun	1 Kings 12:1-13:10	John 21	Ps. 94:1-11
16-Jun	1 Kings 13:11-14:31	Acts 1:1-11	Ps. 94:12-23
17-Jun	1 Kings 15:1-16:20	Acts 1:12-26	Ps. 95
18-Jun	1 Kings 16:21-18:19	Acts 2:1-21	Ps. 96:1-8
19-Jun	1 Kings 18:20-19:21	Acts 2:22-41	Ps. 96:9-13
20-Jun	1 Kings 20	Acts 2:42-3:26	Ps. 97:1-6
21-Jun	1 Kings 21:1-22:28	Acts 4:1-22	Ps. 97:7-12
22-Jun	1 Kings 22:29- 2 Kings 1:18	Acts 4:23-5:11	Ps. 98
23-Jun	2 Kings 2-3	Acts 5:12-28	Ps. 99

24-Jun	2 Kings 4	Acts 5:29-6:15	Ps. 100
25-Jun	2 Kings 5:1-6:23	Acts 7:1-16	Ps. 101
26-Jun	2 Kings 6:24-8:15	Acts 7:17-36	Ps. 102:1-7
27-Jun	2 Kings 8:16-9:37	Acts 7:37-53	Ps. 102:8-17
28-Jun	2 Kings 10-11	Acts 7:54-8:8	Ps. 102:18-28
29-Jun	2 Kings 12-13	Acts 8:9-40	Ps. 103:1-9
30-Jun	2 Kings 14-15	Acts 9:1-16	Ps. 103:10-14
1-Jul	2 Kings 16-17	Acts 9:17-31	Ps. 103:15-22
2-Jul	2 Kings 18:1-19:7	Acts 9:32-10:16	Ps. 104:1-9
3-Jul	2 Kings 19:8-20:21	Acts 10:17-33	Ps. 104:10-23
4-Jul	2 Kings 21:1-22:20	Acts 10:34-11:18	Ps. 104: 24-30
5-Jul	2 Kings 23	Acts 11:19-12:17	Ps. 104:31-35
6-Jul	2 Kings 24-25	Acts 12:18-13:13	Ps. 105:1-7
7-Jul	1 Chron. 1-2	Acts 13:14-43	Ps. 105:8-15
8-Jul	1 Chron. 3:1-5:10	Acts 13:44-14:10	Ps. 105:16-28
9-Jul	1 Chron. 5:11-6:81	Acts 14:11-28	Ps. 105:29-36
10-Jul	1 Chron. 7:1-9:9	Acts 15:1-18	Ps. 105:37-45
11-Jul	1 Chron. 9:10-11:9	Acts 15:19-41	Ps. 106:1-12
12-Jul	1 Chron. 11:10-12:40	Acts 16:1-15	Ps. 106:13-27
13-Jul	1 Chron. 13-15	Acts 16:16-40	Ps. 106:28-33
14-Jul	1 Chron. 16-17	Acts 17:1-14	Ps. 106:34-43
15-Jul	1 Chron. 18-20	Acts 17:15-34	Ps. 106:44-48
16-Jul	1 Chron. 21-22	Acts 18:1-23	Ps. 107:1-9
17-Jul	1 Chron. 23-25	Acts 18:24-19:10	Ps. 107:10-16
18-Jul	1 Chron. 26-27	Acts 19:11-22	Ps. 107:17-32
19-Jul	1 Chron. 28-29	Acts 19:23-41	Ps. 107:33-38
20-Jul	2 Chron. 1-3	Acts 20:1-16	Ps. 107:39-43
21-Jul	2 Chron. 4:1-6:11	Acts 20:17-38	Ps. 108
22-Jul	2 Chron. 6:12-7:10	Acts 21:1-14	Ps. 109:1-20
23-Jul	2 Chron. 7:11-9:28	Acts 21:15-32	Ps. 109:21-31
24-Jul	2 Chron. 9:29-12:16	Acts 21:33-22:16	Ps. 110:1-3
25-Jul	2 Chron. 13-15	Acts 22:17-23:11	Ps. 110:4-7
26-Jul	2 Chron. 16-17	Acts 23:12-24:21	Ps. 111
27-Jul	2 Chron. 18-19	Acts 24:22-25:12	Ps. 112
28-Jul	2 Chron. 20-21	Acts 25:13-27	Ps. 113
29-Jul	2 Chron. 22-23	Acts 26	Ps. 114
30-Jul	2 Chron. 24:1-25:16	Acts 27:1-20	Ps. 115:1-10
31-Jul	2 Chron. 25:17-27:9	Acts 27:21-28:6	Ps. 115:11-18
1-Aug	2 Chron. 28:1-29:19	Acts 28:7-31	Ps. 116:1-5
2-Aug	2 Chron. 29:20-30:27	Rom. 1:1-17	Ps. 116:6-19
3-Aug	2 Chron. 31-32	Rom. 1:18-32	Ps. 117
4-Aug	2 Chron. 33:1-34:7	Rom. 2	Ps. 118:1-18
5-Aug	2 Chron. 34:8-35:19	Rom. 3:1-26	Ps. 118:19-23
6-Aug	2 Chron. 35:20-36:23	Rom. 3:27-4:25	Ps. 118:24-29

7-Aug	Ezra 1-3	Rom. 5	Ps. 119:1-8
8-Aug	Ezra 4-5	Rom. 6:1-7:6	Ps. 119:9-16
9-Aug	Ezra 6:1-7:26	Rom. 7:7-25	Ps. 119:17-32
10-Aug	Ezra 7:27-9:4	Rom. 8:1-27	Ps. 119:33-40
11-Aug	Ezra 9:5-10:44	Rom. 8:28-39	Ps. 119:41-64
12-Aug	Neh. 1:1-3:16	Rom. 9:1-18	Ps. 119:65-72
13-Aug	Neh. 3:17-5:13	Rom. 9:19-33	Ps. 119:73-80
14-Aug	Neh. 5:14-7:73	Rom. 10:1-13	Ps. 119:81-88
15-Aug	Neh. 8:1-9:5	Rom. 10:14-11:24	Ps. 119:89-104
16-Aug	Neh. 9:6-10:27	Rom. 11:25-12:8	Ps. 119:105-120
17-Aug	Neh. 10:28-12:26	Rom. 12:9-13:7	Ps. 119:121-128
18-Aug	Neh. 12:27-13:31	Rom. 13:8-14:12	Ps. 119:129-136
19-Aug	Esther 1:1-2:18	Rom. 14:13-15:13	Ps. 119:137-152
20-Aug	Esther 2:19-5:14	Rom. 15:14-21	Ps. 119:153-168
21-Aug	Esther. 6-8	Rom. 15:22-33	Ps. 119:169-176
22-Aug	Esther 9-10	Rom. 16	Ps. 120-122
23-Aug	Job 1-3	1 Cor. 1:1-25	Ps. 123
24-Aug	Job 4-6	1 Cor. 1:26-2:16	Ps. 124-125
25-Aug	Job 7-9	1 Cor. 3	Ps. 126-127
26-Aug	Job 10-13	1 Cor. 4:1-13	Ps. 128-129
27-Aug	Job 14-16	1 Cor. 4:14-5:13	Ps. 130
28-Aug	Job 17-20	1 Cor. 6	Ps. 131
29-Aug	Job 21-23	1 Cor. 7:1-16	Ps. 132
30-Aug	Job 24-27	1 Cor. 7:17-40	Ps. 133-134
31-Aug	Job 28-30	1 Cor. 8	Ps. 135
1-Sep	Job 31-33	1 Cor. 9:1-18	Ps. 136:1-9
2-Sep	Job 34-36	1 Cor. 9:19-10:13	Ps. 136:10-26
3-Sep	Job 37-39	1 Cor. 10:14-11:1	Ps. 137
4-Sep	Job 40-42	1 Cor. 11:2-34	Ps. 138
5-Sep	Eccles. 1:1-3:15	1 Cor. 12:1-26	Ps. 139:1-6
6-Sep	Eccles. 3:16-6:12	1 Cor. 12:27-13:13	Ps. 139:7-18
7-Sep	Eccles. 7:1-9:12	1 Cor. 14:1-22	Ps. 139:19-24
8-Sep	Eccles. 9:13-12:14	1 Cor. 14:23-15:11	Ps. 140:1-8
9-Sep	SS 1-4	1 Cor. 15:12-34	Ps. 140:9-13
10-Sep	SS 5-8	1 Cor. 15:35-58	Ps. 141
11-Sep	Isa. 1-2	1 Cor. 16	Ps. 142
12-Sep	Isa. 3-5	2 Cor. 1:1-11	Ps. 143:1-6
13-Sep	Isa. 6-8	2 Cor. 1:12-2:4	Ps. 143:7-12
14-Sep	Isa. 9-10	2 Cor. 2:5-17	Ps. 144
15-Sep	Isa. 11-13	2 Cor. 3	Ps. 145
16-Sep	Isa. 14-16	2 Cor. 4	Ps. 146
17-Sep	Isa. 17-19	2 Cor. 5	Ps. 147:1-11
18-Sep	Isa. 20-23	2 Cor. 6	Ps. 147:12-20
19-Sep	Isa. 24:1-26:19	2 Cor. 7	Ps. 148

20-Sep	Isa. 26:20-28:29	2 Cor. 8	Ps. 149-150
21-Sep	Isa. 29-30	2 Cor. 9	Prov. 1:1-9
22-Sep	Isa. 31-33	2 Cor. 10	Prov. 1:10-22
23-Sep	Isa. 34-36	2 Cor. 11	Prov. 1:23-26
24-Sep	Isa. 37-38	2 Cor. 12:1-10	Prov. 1:27-33
25-Sep	Isa. 39-40	2 Cor. 12:11-13:14	Prov. 2:1-15
26-Sep	Isa. 41-42	Gal. 1	Prov. 2:16-22
27-Sep	Isa. 43:1-44:20	Gal. 2	Prov. 3:1-12
28-Sep	Isa. 44:21-46:13	Gal. 3:1-18	Prov. 3:13-26
29-Sep	Isa. 47:1-49:13	Gal 3:19-29	Prov. 3:27-35
30-Sep	Isa. 49:14-51:23	Gal 4:1-11	Prov. 4:1-19
1-Oct	Isa. 52-54	Gal. 4:12-31	Prov. 4:20-27
2-Oct	Isa. 55-57	Gal. 5	Prov. 5:1-14
3-Oct	Isa. 58-59	Gal. 6	Prov. 5:15-23
4-Oct	Isa. 60-62	Eph. 1	Prov. 6:1-5
5-Oct	Isa. 63:1-65:16	Eph. 2	Prov. 6:6-19
6-Oct	Isa. 65:17-66:24	Eph. 3:1-4:16	Prov. 6:20-26
7-Oct	Jer. 1-2	Eph. 4:17-32	Prov. 6:27-35
8-Oct	Jer. 3:1-4:22	Eph. 5	Prov. 7:1-5
9-Oct	Jer. 4:23-5:31	Eph. 6	Prov. 7:6-27
10-Oct	Jer. 6:1-7:26	Phil. 1:1-26	Prov. 8:1-11
11-Oct	Jer. 7:26-9:16	Phil. 1:27-2:18	Prov. 8:12-21
12-Oct	Jer. 9:17-11:17	Phil. 2:19-30	Prov. 8:22-36
13-Oct	Jer. 11:18-13:27	Phil. 3	Prov. 9:1-6
14-Oct	Jer. 14-15	Phil. 4	Prov. 9:7-18
15-Oct	Jer. 16-17	Col. 1:1-23	Prov. 10:1-5
16-Oct	Jer. 18:1-20:6	Col. 1:24-2:15	Prov. 10:6-14
17-Oct	Jer. 20:7-22:19	Col. 2:16-3:4	Prov. 10:15-26
18-Oct	Jer. 22:20-23:40	Col. 3:5-4:1	Prov. 10:27-32
19-Oct	Jer. 24-25	Col. 4:2-18	Prov. 11:1-11
20-Oct	Jer. 26-27	1 Thes. 1:1-2:8	Prov. 11:12-21
21-Oct	Jer. 28-29	1 Thes. 2:9-3:13	Prov. 11:22-26
22-Oct	Jer. 30:1-31:22	1 Thes. 4:1-5:11	Prov. 11:27-31
23-Oct	Jer. 31:23-32:35	1 Thes. 5:12-28	Prov. 12:1-14
24-Oct	Jer. 32:36-34:7	2 Thes. 1-2	Prov. 12:15-20
25-Oct	Jer. 34:8-36:10	2 Thes. 3	Prov. 12:21-28
26-Oct	Jer. 36:11-38:13	1 Tim. 1:1-17	Prov. 13:1-4
27-Oct	Jer. 38:14-40:6	1 Tim. 1:18-3:13	Prov. 13:5-13
28-Oct	Jer. 40:7-42:22	1 Tim. 3:14-4:10	Prov. 13:14-21
29-Oct	Jer. 43-44	1 Tim. 4:11-5:16	Prov. 13:22-25
30-Oct	Jer. 45-47	1 Tim. 5:17-6:21	Prov. 14:1-6
31-Oct	Jer. 48:1-49:6	2 Tim. 1	Prov. 14:7-22
1-Nov	Jer. 49:7-50:16	2 Tim. 2	Prov. 14:23-27
2-Nov	Jer. 50:17-51:14	2 Tim. 3	Prov. 14:28-35

3-Nov	Jer. 51:15-64	2 Tim. 4	Prov. 15:1-9
4-Nov	Jer. 52-Lam. 1	Ti. 1:1-9	Prov. 15:10-17
5-Nov	Lam. 2:1-3:38	Ti. 1:10-2:15	Prov. 15:18-26
6-Nov	Lam. 3:39-5:22	Ti. 3	Prov. 15:27-33
7-Nov	Ezek. 1:1-3:21	Philemon 1	Prov. 16:1-9
8-Nov	Ezek. 3:22-5:17	Heb. 1:1-2:4	Prov. 16:10-21
9-Nov	Ezek. 6-7	Heb. 2:5-18	Prov. 16:22-33
10-Nov	Ezek. 8-10	Heb. 3:1-4:3	Prov. 17:1-5
11-Nov	Ezek. 11-12	Heb. 4:4-5:10	Prov. 17:6-12
12-Nov	Ezek. 13-14	Heb. 5:11-6:20	Prov. 17:13-22
13-Nov	Ezek. 15:1-16:43	Heb. 7:1-28	Prov. 17:23-28
14-Nov	Ezek. 16:44-17:24	Heb. 8:1-9:10	Prov. 18:1-7
15-Nov	Ezek. 18-19	Heb. 9:11-28	Prov. 18:8-17
16-Nov	Ezek. 20	Heb. 10:1-25	Prov. 18:18-24
17-Nov	Ezek. 21-22	Heb. 10:26-39	Prov. 19:1-8
18-Nov	Ezek. 23	Heb. 11:1-31	Prov. 19:9-14
19-Nov	Ezek. 24-26	Heb. 11:32-40	Prov. 19:15-21
20-Nov	Ezek. 27-28	Heb. 12:1-13	Prov. 19:22-29
21-Nov	Ezek. 29-30	Heb. 12:14-29	Prov. 20:1-18
22-Nov	Ezek. 31-32	Heb. 13	Prov. 20:19-24
23-Nov	Ezek. 33:1-34:10	Jas. 1	Prov. 20:25-30
24-Nov	Ezek. 34:11-36:15	Jas. 2	Prov. 21:1-8
25-Nov	Ezek. 36:16-37:28	Jas. 3	Prov. 21:9-18
26-Nov	Ezek. 38-39	Jas. 4:1-5:6	Prov. 21:19-24
27-Nov	Ezek. 40	Jas. 5:7-20	Prov. 21:25-31
28-Nov	Ezek. 41:1-43:12	1 Pet. 1:1-12	Prov. 22:1-9
29-Nov	Ezek. 43:13-44:31	1 Pet. 1:13-2:3	Prov. 22:10-23
30-Nov	Ezek. 45-46	1 Pet. 2:4-17	Prov. 22:24-29
1-Dec	Ezek. 47-48	1 Pet. 2:18-3:7	Prov. 23:1-9
2-Dec	Dan. 1:1-2:23	1 Pet. 3:8-4:19	Prov. 23:10-16
3-Dec	Dan. 2:24-3:30	1 Pet. 5	Prov. 23:17-25
4-Dec	Dan. 4	2 Pet. 1	Prov. 23:26-35
5-Dec	Dan. 5	2 Pet. 2	Prov. 24:1-18
6-Dec	Dan. 6:1-7:14	2 Pet. 3	Prov. 24:19-27
7-Dec	Dan. 7:15-8:27	1 John 1:1-2:17	Prov. 24:28-34
8-Dec	Dan. 9-10	1 John 2:18-29	Prov. 25:1-12
9-Dec	Dan. 11-12	1 John 3:1-12	Prov. 25:13-17
10-Dec	Hos. 1-3	1 John 3:13-4:16	Prov. 25:18-28
11-Dec	Hos. 4-6	1 John 4:17-5:21	Prov. 26:1-16
12-Dec	Hos. 7-10	2 John	Prov. 26:17-21
13-Dec	Hos. 11-14	3 John	Prov. 26:22-27:9
14-Dec	Joel 1:1-2:17	Jude	Prov. 27:10-17
15-Dec	Joel 2:18-3:21	Rev. 1:1-2:11	Prov. 27:18-27
16-Dec	Amos 1:1-4:5	Rev. 2:12-29	Prov. 28:1-8